Praise for *The Show Must Go On*

"Les Goldberg's best book yet! An enjoyable read with good content and great wisdom. An essential reference for business leaders."

Huntly Christie, CEO
Christie Lites

"If you want to know a recipe for success, just read *The Show Must Go On*. The dynamo that is Les Goldberg is an extraordinary leader. He knows where he wants to go, clearly defines the goals, and encourages and nurtures his team to ensure everyone comes along for the ride. The success LMG has experienced isn't by accident!"

Peter Worth, Managing Director
Audio Visual Dynamics

"A wonderful summary and reminder of what good leadership is and should be all about. I especially enjoyed the combination of Les' personal experiences from our industry combined with 'Leadership in Action' insights featuring a fascinating collection of leaders throughout history."

Nico Ubenauf, CEO
satis&fy AG

"*The Show Must Go On* is a master class in leadership and crisis management through the COVID-19 pandemic. It presents a best practices approach to survive and thrive in times of crisis. With my professional sports background, I'm hard-wired to appreciate information in a playbook format designed to win. *The Show Must Go On* will be required reading for our management team!"

Tony McGee, Owner,
HNM Global Logistics, former NFL player

The Show Must Go On

Books by Les M. Goldberg

Don't Take No for an Answer: Anything is Possible

When All the Stars Align: Create a Life Where Great Things Happen

The Show Must Go On

The Art of Leading Through a Crisis

Les M. Goldberg

Courage to Dream Media
2350 Investors Row
Orlando, FL 32837

This publication is designed to provide accurate and authoritative information in regard to the subject matter covered. It is sold with the understanding that the publisher and author are not engaged in rendering legal, accounting or other professional services. If legal advice or other expert assistance is required, the services of a competent professional person should be sought.

The Show Must Go On: The Art of Leading Through a Crisis / Les M. Goldberg

ISBN 978-0-9963548-4-4 Hardcover
ISBN 978-0-9963548-5-1 Paperback
ISBN 978-0-9963548-6-8 Ebook

For the incredibly hard-working individuals with
Entertainment Technology Partners who overcame
a two-year shutdown of the live events business and
emerged stronger than ever.
Thank you.

CONTENTS

Author's Note

Crises are some of life's best teachers. They help us learn how to make quick decisions, take effective action, and do better next time.

A crisis is a time of intense difficulty, trouble or danger when important choices must be made and critical strategies developed and implemented quickly, often with incomplete information. In any ranking of crises, the COVID-19 pandemic is at the top. Those of us who led companies through that chaotic time received an advanced education in the process.

I've been developing my leadership skills since I was a teenager. I believe it's essential to always be learning and growing. Though I never thought I knew it all, I also didn't know how much I would learn when an invisible virus attacked the world and changed the people gathering industry forever. The lessons came fast and furious in the form of new challenges and unique obstacles.

This is not just another pandemic survival story and it's more than just another leadership book. It's a book about mountains and valleys, about pain and exhilaration, about succeeding in the face of insurmountable odds. It's a book about developing the drive and determination to roll with the punches and get back on your feet.

Most important, it's a book of real-life crisis leadership lessons that can be applied to any organization.

LMG, the company I started when I was in high school, delivers state-of-the-art show technology to clients around the world.

In 2014, I formed Entertainment Technology Partners (ETP) as a parent company to a collection of exceptional brands in the industry. I wanted to help like-minded companies in our industry succeed by sharing combined resources while preserving their individual identities and entrepreneurial spirits.

LMG and ETP are recognized leaders in the multibillion-dollar global event industry. We've been able to achieve and maintain this position because we know what it takes to make the show happen and we know that, no matter what, the show must go on.

Les M. Goldberg

CHAPTER ONE

WE DIDN'T SEE THIS COMING

I remember spending the weekend in New Smyrna Beach in April 2020. It was the early days of the COVID pandemic. Everything had shut down, and we were all trying to make sense of what was happening.

As I stood on the shore watching the foamy water rush across the sand, I realized the ocean is a metaphor for business. The sand, the vegetation, the amazing sea life—it's always the same and yet ever-changing. Sometimes the waves are quiet and gentle, sometimes they come crashing violently to the shore. Even as the surface view is familiar, so much remains unknown—we can only guess about what's below. In fact, New Smyrna Beach is known as the shark bite capital of the world and we never know what's lurking out of sight under the waves, waiting to attack.

From my view overlooking the massive, mysterious Atlantic, I reflected on what had just happened. Coming out of 2019, the economy was booming. Unemployment was the lowest it had been in dcades. The stock market was roaring. It seemed as though we could do nothing wrong.

Then we woke up one morning and someone turned off the power. We were at war with a microscopic organism that we couldn't see, we couldn't taste, and we didn't understand. Hotels and convention centers went from packed to empty overnight. Theaters and concert halls went dark. Live events, the core of our business, shut down. People were afraid. Panic and hysteria became the norm.

We'd never seen or felt anything like it.

LMG has been a recognized leader in the people gathering business for decades and we've worked at every level. Our teams stage shows in the largest convention centers in the world, in landmark arenas, and in smaller but stunning venues across the globe. We know our business, and we know how to stage awe-inspiring events using technology and imagination. But a pandemic wasn't something we'd gone to school for. There were no classes we could take, no operations manual to tell us what to do when a pandemic shut the world down. We had to learn how to survive in a new environment.

Sure, I'd faced tough times before. After nearly four decades in business, my survival skills are pretty sharp. But they were about to be tested in a way no one could have imagined.

I'm a pragmatic optimist. I know you don't win every battle. Especially in the people-gathering business, no matter how much you prepare, how much you do right, there will be things beyond your control that will go wrong. And when they do, you deal with them as best you can. The key is preservation. You do what's necessary to keep the business functioning. When you get knocked down, get up and keep going. I'm known for tackling crises like equipment failures and transportation delays with the attitude of, "Nobody died. Whatever happens, it will be okay."

But suddenly, people were dying. Hundreds of thousands of them, all over the world. Businesses were closing. Lifestyles were changing. As a leader, I had to figure out how to run my company in a world I had never imagined. I was faced with decisions that were difficult and painful to make and implement.

That first year of the pandemic was exhilarating and

excruciating. But even as I watched companies, some owned by close friends, close their doors forever, there was never a doubt in my mind that ETP would survive. We're different now, of course. We made some mistakes. But we're strong, flexible, and resilient. Our team has proven itself time and time again, and continues to function with amazing clarity and purpose.

It's been an adventure I could never have predicted, packed with lessons I didn't know I needed to learn. The lessons are still coming every day, and I'm still learning every day. It's a privilege to share that journey with you now.

CHAPTER TWO

THE CAPTAIN OF THE TEAM

W hen times are good, it's easy to be in charge. Decisions aren't difficult. Mistakes aren't hard to fix. Leading still takes effort, but there's plenty of room for error when the economy is roaring, you're growing, you've got a great team on board, and profit margins are strong.

When times get challenging, so does being a leader. And in a crisis, great leadership is not optional, it's a requirement. Without great leadership, teams flounder, organizations fall apart, and businesses fail.

Great leaders step up in times of crises. They make the tough decisions, the gut-wrenching decisions, the decisions that impact the lives of people they'll never know. It's not easy—in fact, it's often agonizing. But once a decision is made, they do what has to be done; they don't second-guess themselves. They know they're on a bus that's heading for a cliff and they can't get off, so they have to stop the bus from disaster.

I'm talking about being a leader, not leadership styles. Of course, leadership styles are important, and it helps to understand them. In 1939, a team of researchers led by German-American psychologist Kurt Lewin determined that there were three basic leadership styles: authoritarian (autocratic), participative (democratic), and delegative (laissez-faire). Since then, experts have identified other styles of leadership, including transformational, situational, charismatic, transactional, pacesetter, bureaucratic, coach, and servant. Most leaders will blend two or more of these styles, depending on the situation and what's needed. I think the best business leaders are ones that encourage their people to make decisions and be accountable for them (that's how you develop new leaders), but in the end, it's not the style that's important, it's the results. We know great leadership when we see it. We also recognize poor leadership.

When they're in the early days of their businesses, entrepreneurs typically don't give much conscious thought to leadership. They're in love with what they're doing, and they lead intuitively and instinctively. As the business grows, they become more intentional about leadership, more aware of its importance in their success. They learn that leadership and management are not the same. Both functions are critical, but they require different skills.

Leadership is about charting the course—Where are we going? How are we going to get there? What is everyone going to contribute?—and then making sure we arrive at our destination with everyone on board.

The best and simplest illustration of leadership is the coxswain in rowing. From where they sit in the bow or stern of the boat, they control the boat's steering, speed, timing, and fluidity. In a race, they motivate the crew and steer as straight a course as possible to make the distance to the finish line as short as possible. Another is an orchestra conductor. They stand there with their baton, telling all the musicians what to do, keeping them playing the right notes at the right time so they create a beautiful melody and not just a jarring sound.

As a leader, you're trying to build a winning team and execute a plan that serves the organization's mission. To do that, you have to get everyone involved working with you and each other. You have to get them aligned, moving in the same direction, blending their efforts to achieve the goal. Each person has to know what they have to do and when. They have to be collectively agile and responsive. And they have to trust the others on their team.

Making that happen is the leader's top priority.

It's all about the team

The leader is a member of the team, not set apart or above it. Each member of the team has a role to play and they're all important, from the warehouse workers to the executives. Those aren't just pretty words, that's reality. To be effective, leaders must understand and respect that.

ETP has a casual environment. Everyone is on a first-name basis. And while we have positions with appropriate titles and responsibilities (director, manager, supervisor, etc.), we're all working together to get the job done. Once, when a member of our leadership team brought his son to work, he introduced me, saying, "This is my boss." I immediately corrected him. I said, "No, no, no. We work together."

There's value in building people up, especially in front of their families. I do it whenever I have the opportunity—and it's not just lip service. A great deal of the work I do supports the people who are dealing with the customers in administrative and technical roles. They're the superstars, not me. Those people are critical to the mission of the company; it's something that's been ingrained in me from the beginning.

Do I make key financial decisions? Sure. Someone has to. It's my job. Are there certain levels of corporate actions that require my approval? Of course. That's my job, too. Am I involved in every sale or purchase negotiation? Every show? Every musical tour? Every installation? No. We have teams of people whose job it is to do those things. The company employs them and they work for whatever motivates them individually (satisfaction, recognition, money, etc.). We'll talk more about motivation in Chapter 8. What I'm talking about here is the role of the leader within the team.

As the leader, I often *get* credit for what the team does, but I don't *take* credit for it. This is an important distinction. When the

Leadership in Action: Colin Powell

Born in Harlem to Jamaican immigrant parents, Colin Powell joined the Reserve Officers' Training Corps (ROTC) while attending college and was a professional soldier for 35 years, rising to the rank of general. His last assignment was as the 12th chairman of the Joint Chiefs of Staff, the highest military position in the Department of Defense. He served as Secretary of State under President George W. Bush from 2001 to 2005.

Powell's legacy includes these thirteen rules of leadership:

1. It ain't as bad as you think! It will look better in the morning.
2. Get mad then get over it.
3. Avoid having your ego so close to your position that when your position falls, your ego goes with it.
4. It can be done.
5. Be careful what you choose. You may get it.
6. Don't let adverse facts stand in the way of a good decision.
7. You can't make someone else's choices. You shouldn't let someone else make yours.
8. Check small things.
9. Share credit.
10. Remain calm. Be kind.
11. Have a vision. Be demanding.
12. Don't take counsel of your fears or naysayers.
13. Perpetual optimism is a force multiplier.

goal is met, a smart leader gives credit to the team and, when appropriate, to specific individuals. If the goal is missed, the leader is ultimately responsible. We see that in professional sports all the time. When a team of highly skilled athletes doesn't win, the players aren't the ones who get fired (although some of them might get traded), it's the coach who gets the ax.

In business, when someone on the team makes a mistake, the leader has two primary functions. One is to guide the team in developing and executing the plan to correct the mistake; the other is to deal with the customer, which sometimes means taking flak. When some people are unhappy, they need to express their frustration to the highest level person in the organization they can reach, and it's important to let them vent.

In the early days of the pandemic as we were transitioning from in-person to virtual events, we did an event for a long-time customer, one who had been with us for decades. We made a small but serious mistake—one of our technicians forgot to push a button. Missing that one little mouse click meant we didn't record the audio for one of the presenters. We had video but no sound.

Disappointing one of my best customers was a crushing blow to me personally and taking responsibility for it was not fun. But I wasn't going to throw the technician under the bus. What we had to do was fix the mistake and put safeguards in place so it wouldn't happen again.

The only thing we could do was re-record the session and do everything we could to make minimize the inconvenience to the presenter. Unfortunately, the presenter was not using a script and we needed to duplicate what he said. Someone on the team came up with the brilliant idea of sending the video to a lip reader who could create a transcript without hearing the presenter. At the time, I had no idea this was even possible, but I'm thankful someone on my team did. The lip reader was able to create a written transcript for the presenter to read and we were ultimately able to deliver a good video of the presentation. And even while we were still in the process of doing that, we were also putting systems and safeguards in place so something like that can never happen again.

Just as leaders hold people accountable, they are accountable. President Harry S. Truman was known for the sign on his desk that said, "The buck stops here." The phrase comes from the slang expression "pass the buck," which means to pass the responsibility to someone else. In his farewell address when he left office, Truman said:

> *"The President—whoever he is—has to decide. He can't pass the buck to anybody. No one else can do the deciding for him. That's his job."*

This applies to any leader. When you're the leader, the buck stops with you. It's your responsibility, whether you're the coach of a sports team, the manager of a department, the owner of the company, or the President of the United States.

To be an effective leader at any level, you must be respected by your team. You must have a plan. You must be able to navigate shark-infested waters. You must be able to deal with obstacles. And you must have a positive outlook.

YOUR ATTITUDE IS YOUR TOP PRIORITY

I believe a positive attitude is the single most important quality for anyone to have, but it's especially important for leaders. As a leader, you have to believe that you can overcome any challenge, no matter what it is. You have to believe you're going to ultimately win. If you don't, you need to step aside and let someone who does believe take over.

You must, of course, balance your optimism with a healthy dose of realism. Vice Admiral James Stockdale spent more than seven years as a prisoner of war in Vietnam's infamous "Hanoi Hilton". About that time, Stockdale said:

> *"I never lost faith in the end of the story. I never doubted not only that I would get out, but also that I would prevail in the end and turn the experience into the defining event of my life, which, in retrospect, I would not trade."*

Jim Collins interviewed Stockdale for his book, *Good to Great: Why Some Companies Make the Leap…and Others Don't.* When Collins asked about the men who didn't make it out alive, Stockdale said:

> *"The optimists. They were the ones who said: 'We're going to be out by Christmas.' And Christmas would come, and Christmas would go. Then they'd say: 'We're going to be out by Easter.' And Easter would come, and Easter would go. And then Thanksgiving, and then it would be Christmas again. And they died of a broken heart. This is a very important lesson. You must never confuse faith that you will prevail in the end—which you can never afford to lose—with the discipline to confront the most brutal facts of your current reality, whatever they might be."*

It's the ability to face reality with a positive attitude that helps leaders win the war, even if they lose an occasional battle. Negativity drags everyone down and is a recipe for guaranteed failure. Not only will being negative damage your business, it can make you physically ill.

Having a positive attitude is more than chanting affirmations and whistling a happy tune. It's being optimistic and expecting the best. It's seeing the good in people. It's being confident of your ability to deal with whatever situations and challenges arise. It's being able to bounce back from disappointments and failures. It's making lemonade when life hands you lemons.

A big part of a positive attitude is being happy—but when you're the leader, you're the last person in the process who gets to be made happy. An entrepreneur knows the organization's priorities. Are we here to serve our customers? Are we here to serve our employees? Are we here to serve ownership?

When it comes to those three questions, I can tell you that as the owner, I'm at the bottom of that food chain. The top of the chain is a tie between my customers and my employees. I realize that if I don't keep our employees happy, they won't keep our customers happy. If our customers aren't happy, they'll take their business somewhere else. So happy customers and happy employees are an equal priority, and unless that happens, I don't get to be happy.

I want everyone to be happy. Life's too short to spend time being unhappy. I perform better when I'm happy—we all do. And I've learned that the best way to be happy is to make others happy. I make a conscious effort to create a great upward spiral of happiness for everyone in my world.

Recently Jamin Brahmbhatt, MD, a friend and client, sent me a text that included a picture of him and the crew that worked on his event. The crew made his show amazing. He wrote:

> *"You, my friend, have an amazing team. You can see your leadership firsthand in their commitment to excellence. Thank you for everything. The meeting was a huge success. We set a new standard."*

He was happy and that made me and our crew happy. Happiness is contagious.

Messages like that one come from our clients regularly and I make sure they're shared with the team members involved. Once in a while, we get a note about something that was not so amazing, and when that happens, we deal with it appropriately. But my point is that a positive attitude and positive reinforcement works—it keeps people motivated and happy and eager to do their best. People want to take pride in their work, they want to be part of a team they're proud of. That level of performance starts with a positive attitude. When leaders have a positive attitude, it's infectious. When they

Leadership in Action: Theodore Roosevelt, Jr.

Often referred to as Teddy or T.R., Theodore Roosevelt had a blend of courage and compassion that made him a model leader for his time and the generations to come. He became the U.S.'s youngest president when he assumed office at the age of 42 following the assassination of William McKinley. Some of his most effective achievements were in conservation.

Though he was born into privilege, his life included struggles, tragedies, and failures.

He believed in learning from the past.

"It is of little use for us to pay lip-loyalty to the mighty men of the past unless we sincerely endeavor to apply to the problems of the present precisely the qualities which in other crises enabled the men of that day to meet those crises."

He believed in action.

"In every such crisis the temptation to indecision, to non-action, is great, for excuses can always be found for non-action, and action means risk and the certainty of blame to the man who acts."

He believed in hard work.

"A soft, easy life is not worth living, if it impairs the fiber of brain and heart and muscle. We must dare to be great; and we must realize that greatness is the fruit of toil and sacrifice and high courage... For us is the life of action, of strenuous performance of duty; let us live in the harness, striving mightily; let us rather run the risk of wearing out than rusting out."

He believed in family.

"Home, wife, and children—they are what really count in life."

don't, it's tough to be an effective leader.

SEEING PROBLEMS BEFORE THEY HAPPEN

We expect leaders to find solutions, but they also need to be able to see potential problems before they turn into actual problems. Great leaders watch trends, pay attention to external activity, and have a keen strategic awareness of what is happening and could potentially happen in the future. That lets them get out in front of situations with a plan of action before crisis management becomes necessary.

Most of the problems you'll deal with as a leader won't come as a total surprise. There will usually be signs long before something escalates from issue to crisis. When we debrief after any crisis, we not only evaluate how we handled the situation, we consider whether there were warning signs that we should have paid attention to that might have allowed us to prevent it. If there were, we use that knowledge to avoid similar crises in the future.

Being a "problem visionary" doesn't mean you're a pessimist who is always looking for the worst-case scenario, it means you're a realist. If you smell smoke, you need to go looking for the fire so you can extinguish it before it does a lot of damage.

WATCHING THE LEADERS RISE TO THE TOP

In any group, someone will emerge as the leader. It's a natural process. With juries, the judge doesn't appoint a foreperson; the jurors decide among themselves who that is going to be. Put a group of any size together and tell them to come up with a plan, someone is going to step up and say, "Okay, let's figure this out."

Organizations have one top leader who is supported by many people who are leaders in their areas. Leaders at every level have a responsibility to identify and mentor future leaders, because those future leaders are the people who will take the company through the ups and downs of the years to come. It's not just about making the organization successful, it's about making it sustainable and making everyone in it successful.

It's awesome to see people rise up and become leaders. Margaret Thatcher once said, "People think that at the top there isn't much room. They tend to think of it as an Everest. My message is that there is tons of room at the top." It's up to the top leader in an organization to build a structure that has plenty of room for people with leadership potential.

Identify the people who are motivated, who demonstrate leadership, and who are aligned with the direction and support the mission and values of the company. When you know who those people are, develop them to be the future leaders of your company. We'll talk more about how to do this is Chapter 5.

THE FUTURE OF LEADERSHIP

As I said at the beginning of this chapter, it's easy to lead when times are good. But great leaders don't coast on the good times. They use those times to grow and develop themselves and their teams so that when the challenges come—and they will!—the organization is ready.

What will effective leadership look like in the future? Leaders will:

- Focus on results not activities.
- Create working environments that eliminate micromanaging and empower team members.
- Welcome and reward innovation.
- Encourage coaching and mentoring throughout the organization.
- Identify new talent and develop future leaders.
- Be receptive to new ideas and be willing to change.

- Be a consistent reflection of the organization's mission and values.

An effective leader naturally builds strong leadership in the organization. An ineffective leader weakens the organization because people who have leadership potential will go somewhere else. People look to their leader for direction. As the leader, you have two options: you can lead people off the cliff to failure or you can lead them up the mountain to success.

CHAPTER THREE

FUELED BY IRON WILL

When I first started LMG, which is now a business unit of ETP, it was just me. I was the company. I did everything from sales to delivering the equipment and service for the event to billing and administration. At the time, I had no idea how big the company would become—I was just a kid who was excited by what I was doing, I was willing to work hard and do whatever it took to meet my commitments and keep the customers happy. I was fueled by iron will then, and it's how I operate today.

We have a few contracts with convention centers across the country to provide services to people who use the centers for various types of events. It's a win-win-win—the customers get consistent, quality service; we have a regular flow of business in a familiar environment; and the venue gets a commission on the work we do.

Years ago, a decorating company in one of the convention centers decided they were not going to allow us access to our dedicated docks to load equipment in and out. They wanted all the equipment that hit the show floor to be weighed and measured so they could charge drayage (a per pound rate) to move it from the dock to the exhibit booths. That created an impossible environment for us and our customers. It essentially doubled the price to our customers, it was not good for our business, and the convention center wasn't getting any revenue from the decorator.

We had to go to battle—in the most diplomatic of ways, of course. After almost a year of jumping over an incredible number of hoops and obstacles, we finally got the situation resolved. It took persistence and fortitude. It took iron will.

Iron will is determination. It's not making excuses. It's not giving up. And it's non-negotiable. It's essential for entrepreneurs in their day-to-day activities and especially in a crisis. If you don't have iron will, you'll fail as an entrepreneur and as a leader.

You see iron will in athletes all the time. You see it when a climber approaches the peak of Mount Everest, when a runner hits mile 26 of a marathon, when a weightlifter raises those extra pounds—right there at the end, when they're exhausted and struggling and it would be easy to stop, they keep going. They use every ounce of energy they have and somehow find more so they can finish, so they can break a record or win the competition. This is why athletes typically make great leaders—they have the iron will and self-discipline it takes to get the job done.

Iron will is not limited to super spectacular situations. It's a consistent way of operating. For example, during the pandemic, people were afraid to meet in person, but I'm a face-to-face guy. Zoom, Teams, and WebEx are great tools, but I believe true, meaningful relationships happen in person and I didn't want to give up on that. So even when so many places were shut down, I was still meeting with people—sometimes in the craziest of places. When you're told you can't do something that is so fundamental to how you operate, you have to figure out a way to do it—and that takes iron will.

The story we were taking to our clients at the time was how to approach virtual events and what you can do in studios. People wanted to see it. A lot of those presentations happened on Zoom, but a lot happened in person in spite of the special accommodations we had to make.

Once I met the team from a major client in a park in Minneapolis. It was a huge facility, and it didn't have a street address. The parking area was about a mile away from the picnic table they were using. I hiked with my bag and backpack to make a presentation outside to a group of about a dozen people around a picnic table. Could we have done that online? Probably, but it wouldn't have had the impact a face-to-face meeting did.

I was committed to not letting the pandemic stop me from meeting with clients, from maintaining and building relationships so that we could forge ahead and emerge from the shutdown stronger than ever.

This determination comes from inside. It's the ethos of a person. It comes from the unshakeable belief that you're on the right course and you're fully committed to getting to the finish line, no matter how hard it gets.

REJECT FAILURE

Have you ever wondered: When a company fails, who decides that's going to happen? Failure is not something you plan—no entrepreneur has ever written a business plan that said, "And on this date, we will close our doors because we don't have enough business to sustain our operation." Failure is not a moment in time. It's usually the result of short-term planning and choosing short-term gains over long-term results. Be in it for the long-term because that's where business success is.

During the period of the "great resignation" which began in the second year of the COVID-19 pandemic, we lost some people. Every company did; I'll talk more about that in Chapter 5. But there was one employee who, as he was leaving, told me, "I hope you all survive this."

I was stunned.

It had never entered my mind, not even for a split second, that we might not survive. I didn't work this hard building what I have to stop now. I was focused on what we had to do to adapt to the new business environment we were operating in. I was facing challenges I'd never dealt with before. There were times when I wasn't sure what we were going to do, but never did I think there was a chance that we might fail.

Leadership in Action: Abraham Lincoln

A self-taught lawyer, Abraham Lincoln was elected sixteenth President of the United States in 1860 shortly before the Civil War broke out. What made him such an extraordinary leader during such a challenging time?

He was accessible. In 1861, he spent more time out of the White House than in it. He spent about three-quarters of each day meeting with people, which he considered his best source of information. He had an open-door policy, something that would be impossible today.

He was persuasive. He didn't give orders, he made requests. He offered support and encouragement to his subordinates. Because he treated people with respect, they liked him—and because they liked and respected him, they were willing to follow him.

He challenged the status quo. He embraced change and encouraged innovation. As the only President to patent something (a new method of making grounded boats more buoyant), he rewarded people for trying new things and didn't punish them for failure.

He was open to criticism and debate. He used feedback to correct his mistakes and admitted when he was wrong. W.E.B. DuBois said this about Lincoln: "I love him not because he was perfect but because he was not and yet triumphed."

That's the difference between someone who has iron will and someone who doesn't. People who have iron will have strong survival skills. They may be dreamers—entrepreneurs usually are—but they know how to survive. People who are determined will find a way.

The challenging moments you experience as a leader are the moments that will inspire you in the future. Every single crisis we've gone through as a company has left us stronger and better. You've probably heard that line used in reference to politicians that you should never let a good crisis go to waste. That's a good philosophy for business, but from the perspective that you can turn each crisis into a learning experience that helps you grow as an individual and an organization.

Will you have ideas that don't work? Products that flop? Circumstances you can't control that will test you to your limits and beyond? Of course. But it's not failure if you stay committed, stay determined, and don't give up.

EMBRACE OPPORTUNITY

Successful leaders know how to recognize and embrace genuine opportunities. They know how to evaluate what's in front of them and can tell if it's something that's merely doable versus something that they can knock out of the ballpark—or something that's an unworkable pipe dream.

If you've never picked up a tennis racket but someone told you that you can play in the finals at Wimbledon this year, the reality is that you have no chance. That's not opportunity, it's a disaster. Opportunity is something you actually have the ability to do. Opportunity is when you believe you're up for the task and you can shine when you do it. Opportunity occurs at the intersection of luck and hard work for people who are able to recognize it and take advantage of it.

Sometimes people are blind to opportunity. It's right in front of them and they can't see it. They cling to the way things are, they resist change. And they get left behind. Those people aren't leaders—they aren't even good followers.

Of course, just because something is new doesn't mean it's a good opportunity. And not every opportunity that looks good is going to work out. But if you do your homework, evaluate the risk and reward, and listen to your intuition, you'll enjoy far more wins than losses.

Great leaders know how to see opportunity in problems. When there's a challenge, coming up with a solution requires creativity and innovation which can lead to growth and expansion. This applies whether the problem is internal or external—and often whether it's even recognized. Remember, technology has solved problems we didn't know we had until we had the solution. All too often, people simply live with a problem because they believe there's no other choice. Show them a solution and you're a hero. It all comes down to focusing on what other people need and giving it to them.

Years ago, two producers who worked with a major pharmaceutical company came to us because they wanted to start their own production company and they were trying to figure out how to do it. I and a few members of our leadership team sat down with them to talk it out. The pharmaceutical company was willing to let them continue producing the shows, but as a small start-up, they didn't meet the company's vendor requirements but, of course, we did. But our people were saying we couldn't help them because we don't produce shows—producers are our customers and if we started producing shows we would be in direct competition with our customers.

But I love the entrepreneurial spirit and I wanted to figure out a way to help these two guys. So I told everyone we needed to stop the negativity, stop looking at what we *couldn't* do, and figure out what we *could* do—and we weren't leaving the room until we did.

As soon as I said that, the mood shifted and it took us about fifteen minutes to figure out a solution, which was to sub out the production under LMG/ETP's prime contract. We're not producing the shows so we're not competing with other producers, the pharmaceutical company is getting the production talent they want, and two talented producers are building their own company—everybody wins.

Once we changed our mindset from looking at why we *couldn't* do something to figuring out how we *could* do it, we came up with the solution. Everyone took off their dark glasses and looked for practical possibilities—and we found one. It came through tenacity and some out-of-the-box thinking. As a leader, you have to be the one to shut down the doom-and-gloom attitudes and get people looking for the opportunities.

Another aspect of embracing opportunity comes when you can guide your customers to a solution they didn't know existed. We do this on a regular basis. Sometimes our customers know what they want and have an idea for how to create it, but we know how to help them get even better results. Could we just do what they ask for? Sure, but that's not how we work. We want to give them the absolute best outcome possible, and we know the technology and what it can do. That's why we're always making suggestions and looking for ways to give them more than they expected.

There have been times when we've said, "Hey, we've got this really cool idea, we could do this, but you'd be the first." Somebody has to be first, right? And they go for it because they know we've thought it through and we're not going to suggest something that we're not confident will work. We don't suggest anything that we haven't thoroughly tested and put through simulations in our facilities. And no matter how sure we are, we always have a backup plan in place just in case.

There's also the potential for opportunity when someone tells you no. I don't take no for an answer; I figure out a way to turn that no into a yes. We are serving clients today who said no to me years ago, but I didn't give up on them. They eventually gave us a chance, and we proved ourselves.

Opportunities are sometimes in plain sight, but we don't see them. If you find you're being asked about the same thing over and over, there's probably an opportunity there. And when people are complaining, you've definitely got an opportunity.

Opportunities don't always look like you thought they would. They don't always match the vision that played out in your head beforehand. But keep an open mind because what actually happens can be even better.

GET COMFORTABLE WITH BEING UNCOMFORTABLE

When I say that leaders have to be comfortable being uncomfortable, I'm not talking about the personal development advice to get out of your comfort zone. As important as that is, this is even more critical. As a leader, you'll often deal with uncertainty, unfamiliarity, and other circumstances that will make you uncomfortable. You're the captain of the ship and it won't always be smooth sailing. When you're going through the storms, doing the best you can but still not knowing for sure what's going to happen, you're going to be uncomfortable. Get used to it.

Know how to project cool, calm confidence no matter what's going on inside you. Use the techniques work for you—deep breathing, visualization, mental affirmations, activity, whatever. The point is: Never let them see you sweat. Never show fear. And know that feeling uncomfortable and even anxious is a part of being a leader and you need to be comfortable with it.

Put on your Kevlar suit

When you're the leader, you're always in the spotlight. The stage

Leadership in Action: Bob Iger

Bob Iger was chief executive officer of The Walt Disney Company from 2005 to 2020, leading the company through an amazing turnaround and expansion. In his book, *The Ride of a Lifetime: Lessons Learned from 15 Years as CEO of the Walt Disney Company*, he outlines the core principles that are the foundation of his leadership style. They include:

Optimism. "Optimism in a leader, especially in challenging times, is so vital ... Especially in difficult moments, the people you lead need to feel confident in your ability to focus on what matters, and not to operate from a place of defensiveness and self-preservation...The tone you set as a leader has an enormous effect on the people around you. No one wants to follow a pessimist."

Courage. "I didn't want to be in the business of playing it safe. I wanted to be in the business of creating possibilities for greatness."

Curiosity. "The path to innovation begins with curiosity... Innovate or die."

Fairness. "Strong leadership embodies the fair and decent treatment of people...Nothing is worse to an organization than a culture of fear."

Authenticity. "Truth and authenticity breed respect and trust."

The relentless pursuit of perfection. "This doesn't mean perfectionism at all costs, but it does mean a refusal to accept mediocrity or make excuses for something being 'good enough.'"

Integrity. "True integrity—a sense of knowing who you are and being guided by your own clear sense of right and wrong—is a kind of secret leadership weapon. If you trust your own instincts and treat people with respect, the company will come to represent the values you live by."

you're on will vary in size, depending on whether you're leading a small group or a large organization, but you're still the person who gets the applause or the boos. And the bigger the organization, the larger and harsher the spotlight.

Most people get to make their mistakes in private. Leaders don't. And everyone's a critic. Everyone's a great Monday morning quarterback. The best leaders know this and just keep their Kevlar suits on so the darts people throw at them just bounce off. As Zig Ziglar said, "Don't be distracted by criticism. Remember, the only taste of success some people have is when they take a bite out of you."

Of course, while great leaders ignore the zingers, they know how to receive genuine constructive criticism and they are strong enough to admit it when they're wrong. Elon Musk once sent an email to Tesla managers in which he said that when he gives them explicit directions, they have three ways to proceed: explain why he's wrong, ask for clarification, or "execute the directions." I don't know what happens when someone tells Musk he's wrong, but when it happens to me, I listen.

We all know people who can't accept ever being wrong. They think that because they're in charge, they have to always be right—and they'll insist that they're right even when they're not. Great leaders are humble enough to admit when they get it wrong. They accept responsibility and come up with a plan to deal with the situation.

LONELY AT THE TOP? IT DOESN'T HAVE TO BE

In a 2016 interview in the *The Washington Post*, Apple CEO Tim Cook said, "It's sort of a lonely job. The adage that it's lonely—the CEO job is lonely—is accurate in a lot of ways. I'm not looking for any sympathy. CEOs don't need any sympathy."

He's right. Being the top person in a company can be lonely and leaders don't need sympathy. CEOs choose to be where they are. They enjoy a lot of perks and there are ways to deal with the loneliness.

I've learned how important is it for a leader to keep a distinct line between their personal and professional lives. I have a lot of fun at work and I enjoy the people I work with, but I keep my friends and family separate. I know a lot of successful leaders don't agree, but I've found that's the best way to objectively manage and make difficult decisions that affect people.

The "lonely at the top" saying goes beyond social relationships. It applies to making those tough, gut-wrenching decisions. Sure, good leaders have all the input from all the resources—the executive team, the number-crunchers, and so on—but when it comes down to the final decision, it's theirs.

Think about what it must have been like for Harry Truman to make the decision to drop atomic bombs on Japan. About his reasoning, he wrote, "My object is to save as many American lives as possible but I also have a human feeling for the women and children of Japan." Speaking of himself as President, he said, "And he alone, in all the world, must say yes or no to that awesome, ultimate question, 'Shall we drop the bomb on a living target?'" As a result of his decision, an estimated 140,000-215,000 people died, but World War II ended.

Years later, Truman's grandson, Clifton Daniel, said that when a photographer asked Truman if he had any regrets about his decision, "My grandfather said, 'Hell, yes'. You don't do something like that without thinking about it. He didn't want to have to do it but he felt that he had to, to stop the war and to save both American and Japanese lives."

Truman never tried to deflect responsibility for his decision, and he never apologized for it. Daniel said, "He met Colonel Paul Tibbets [pilot of the *Enola Gay*] after the bombing and asked Tibbets if he was taking any grief from anyone about having used the weapon.

Tibbets said, 'No, I haven't,' and Grandpa said, 'Well, if you do, if anybody gives you a hard time about it, you refer 'em to me because it was my decision. I take responsibility.' So he owned it."

That's what great leaders do. They know their decisions will affect people's lives both in and out of the company, in ways the leaders will see and in ways they may never know. They also know that someone has to make the decision and bear the ultimate responsibility for the results.

Chapter Four

The Decider-in-Chief

W hen you're the captain of the ship, you have to set a course. You don't have the option of going nowhere. You can't say, "We're just going to stand still." The clock is ticking. You must make decisions. Inaction has consequences and they're usually not good.

Strong leaders are strong decision-makers.

Something Dave John, our COO, often says is that the *tough* decision and the *right* decision are usually the same decision. Effective decision-making, especially in a crisis, requires a level of mental toughness that you may not even realize you have.

It concerns me to see people making important decisions too quickly. I think it's good to agonize at least a little bit because it means you're taking the time to really weigh the options. But no matter how easy or hard the process is for you, if you're going to lead, you have to make decisions.

Using triage as a decision-making tool

Decision-making connects all the facts you know to be true to a course of action. It's nice when you have the luxury of time to make important decisions, but that's not always the case. In fact, in today's fast-paced business environment, you rarely have time for leisurely decision-making.

When COVID-19 stopped all the in-person events, we quickly pivoted to virtual shows. People continued to meet, even though they couldn't do it in person, and they needed companies like ETP to help them stage their online meetings. So we didn't stop doing shows, we stopped loading trucks. But changing our systems to bring the same dazzle to virtual events that our customers expected from in-person events took a lot of quick decisions. We had to triage the process.

The term triage comes from the French word "trier" which means to separate, sort, shift, or select. We tend to think of triage in terms of medical treatment in situations where resources are limited and care is prioritized for those who are in most need of immediate attention and would benefit the most from it. Whether we're conscious of it or not, we do triage in business every day, all day long.

The business triage model allocates resources based on priorities and what's available. In a classroom situation, it sounds good to talk about creating a list of necessary tasks, identifying resources, and establishing priorities so work can be implemented. The real world isn't so structured. Especially in a crisis, you have to triage instinctively. You have to assess what's happening right now and make decisions based on the information you have—and it may not be complete. That's one of the biggest challenges of business triage, and it's why you should have a triage system in place before you need it.

A process that will let you quickly get good advice from your team about potential solutions and pathways is essential. Business triage in the real world means gathering your leadership team on a moment's notice, whether it's in-person or online, and coming up with a plan in minutes because you don't have hours or days to think about and research it.

We regularly move equipment around the world for events, most of the time on trucks. We haven't had many truck fires, but there have been a few—and when they happen, they create an emergency. Once, we were shipping equipment from Las Vegas to San Diego for a show. It was a five-hour drive and the truck caught fire about an hour outside Vegas. The trucking company let us know about the fire, but they weren't forthcoming with other details. We didn't know how badly our equipment was damaged. We didn't know exactly where the truck was—if we had, we could have sent another truck to recover our materials. But in the heat of the moment, our priority was to get working equipment to the show site and that's what we focused on. Later, we held a meeting to talk about what happened, where the communications broke down, what we should have done differently, and how we could be better prepared to respond the next time a truck carrying our equipment had a problem. One of the key things we've done is add GPS tracking to everything we ship, so whether our materials are on our own vehicles or a common carrier, we know where they are at all times.

Triage is not the time to assign blame or figure out who is responsible for the problem. It's about keeping the patient alive (and the customer happy) and coming up with a solution for the immediate situation. Clarity on what we could have done better and who is accountable for that comes later.

After every triage situation, once the proverbial (or real) fire is out, take the time to review what happened. Do a postmortem. How was information relayed? Were the decisions effective? What were the lessons that will help you respond better the next time?

KNOW WHO YOUR DECISION-MAKERS ARE

Who are the decision-makers in your organization? You need to know who they are from two key perspectives: the responsibility they hold based on their position in the organization and their natural ability to analyze a situation, come up with a plan, and put it into action.

Decisions should be made at the lowest level possible. When people know how to do things, let them be responsible for those things. Push authority as far down as possible and you'll see your best leaders rise up.

It's important to recognize that some people don't like making decisions. They want to be told what to do. My wife is *not* one of those people, but there are plenty of good workers who are happy with carrying out decisions made by others and they do that well. They might celebrate when things go right, but they don't accept responsibility if

Leadership in Action: Anne Frank

Anne Frank wasn't the head of a company. She was never elected to public office. Beyond her family and friends, no one knew of her until years after her death. But she was a leader.

Even as a youngster, Anne was courageous and optimistic. Her famous diary tells us that she believed in the basic goodness of people and was committed to making a difference in the world. She supported equal rights and wanted to end discrimination.

As a teenager enduring the horrors of Auschwitz, Anne remained sweet and charming. One Auschwitz survivor recalled that Anne remained sensitive and caring when most prisoners protected themselves from feeling anything. Another survivor said of Anne: "We were divided into groups of five … Anne was the youngest in her group, but nevertheless she was the leader of it. She also distributed the bread in the barracks, and she did it so well and fairly that there was none of the usual grumbling."

She didn't tell people what to do. Her leadership manifested in her own behavior. She was then and continues to be a role model for generations past and future through the words in her diary, which include this quote: "Human greatness does not lie in wealth or power, but in character and goodness."

things go wrong because it wasn't their decision. That's okay, as long as everyone understands that those people are not leaders. They're good implementers and you need these people in your organization, but don't expect more from them than they are capable of doing.

You may have people on your team who feel empowered to make decisions to a certain point, but when the situation becomes uncomfortable for them, they elevate it to someone else. They know how much authority and ability they have and they don't exceed it. These people are worth cultivating. Coach them to develop their decision-making skills.

And then you have the strong decision-makers, the people you know you can count on for their judgment whether you're facing a crisis or engaging in long-term planning. These people are your company's most valuable resource.

USE YOUR INTUITION

Albert Einstein once said, "The only real valuable thing is intuition."

Intuition is the ability to know something before you have proof. It's understanding things without conscious reasoning. You might call it instinct, having a gut feeling, a sixth sense. I call it a little birdie inside your head that tells you something is a great idea and something else isn't such a good idea. It's like a mental Ouija board that gives you answers you can't always explain. Whether it's a decision related to your business, your personal life, maybe a medical issue, intuition is that thing that helps you get your arms around your decision.

Strong leaders have strong intuition and mine has served me well. Do you need hard data in business? Of course. But requiring it for every decision will slow you down. You'll stagnate. You can't wait for information that doesn't exist yet to make decisions. That's where intuition comes in. When things just feel right, look right, taste right, you know you can make a decision and take action without all the facts and figures.

The richest source of wisdom is our past experiences, and that's what intuition is built on. Developing your intuition is part of developing yourself as a leader. Start paying attention to those feelings. Track how accurate they are. And let them help you to stay ahead of the competition. The biggest thing that will get in the way of developing and effectively using your intuition is overthinking—playing too many scenarios over and over in your mind, demanding more information, being blocked by what we call the paralysis of analysis. If you find yourself overthinking, stop, clear your mind, focus on yourself, and figure out what you need to take action.

As I explain in Chapter 6, when I take risks, they're calculated risks—and I think that's what most great leaders do. But we have to reconcile calculated risks and intuition. Sometimes my intuition fills in the blanks when I don't have all the data and I need to take a calculated risk. Sometimes my intuition will lead me to take a risk that the information I have at the time doesn't support.

Intuition was definitely at work when Bill Allen, who was CEO of Boeing in the 1950s, convinced his board to risk $16 million on a new transcontinental airliner, the 707. At the time, Boeing was making planes for the defense industry, but Allen had a vision of what the commercial airline industry would eventually become. His calculated risk paid off, and Boeing became the world's leader in the design and production of commercial jets.

When Sony's co-founder Akio Morita invented the Walkman, he wasn't driven by market research. As he watched people play music in their cars and carrying large stereos to parks, his intuition told him there was a market for a truly portable music player that would produce sound like a high-quality car stereo but that was compact and would allow consumers to listen while doing something else. He was right.

At LMG, we use a lot of LED tiles. When we first began building our inventory, we found a U.S.-based company that was selling tiles made in Korea. We thought the company we were dealing with was an exclusive distributor and the manufacturer didn't sell direct. The distributor told us he was only marking the product up ten percent. The price we were quoted seemed reasonable and we were ready to close on the $500,000 deal, but my intuition told me something wasn't right. So I asked a friend of mine in Australia to call the manufacturer and see if he could buy direct and for how much.

The quote was half of the price we were getting ready to pay.

It turned out that the guy we were originally dealing with was *not* an exclusive distributor. And when he found out that we were buying directly from the manufacturer, he went crazy, screaming at us. He wanted to know how we were able to buy the LED tiles and why hadn't we bought them from him. I asked him if he thought a one hundred percent markup (not the ten percent he had claimed) was fair, because I didn't.

We usually buy direct from manufacturers, but occasionally there are situations where it makes sense to go through a distributor. If this guy's price had been ten to fifteen percent higher than the quote my friend had gotten, we probably would have bought from him. But not only was he trying to gouge us, he had misrepresented himself. My intuition told me that, as important as the purchase of those LED tiles was to us, we were dealing with someone who was trying to take advantage of us. I was right.

Here's another example of how intuition has worked for me. We've had an office in Las Vegas since 2001. We built a building in 2007 and in 2018, we decided to expand our facility and put in a production studio. We could have simply expanded the warehouse, which is what we needed, for about $4 million, but I decided to spend another $1 million to add the studio. I didn't have much hard data to back up my decision, but I knew how popular Las Vegas was and that it didn't have a lot of studio space. It's common for the performers in Vegas to need a place for rehearsals or to shoot videos or other projects, so I thought a production studio would get used.

Leadership in Action: Jeff Bezos

Visionary Jeff Bezos founded the now-behemoth that is Amazon in 1994 as an online bookseller, operating out of the garage of his house in Bellevue, Washington. He was motivated by a single projection: that internet usage would go up by 2,300 percent each year.

In his decision-making, Bezos uses what he calls the "Regret Minimization Framework" where he imagines himself in the future, looking back, asking himself if he will regret either doing or not doing what he's considering. That tells him what he needs to do.

Under Bezos' leadership, Amazon became a household name and one of the world's top-valued companies. On its website, the company describes itself this way:

Amazon is guided by four principles: customer obsession rather than competitor focus, passion for invention, commitment to operational excellence, and long-term thinking. Amazon strives to be Earth's most customer-centric company, Earth's best employer, and Earth's safest place to work.

Along with his extraordinary successes, Bezos has had more than his share of failures, and he embraces them. In a letter to Amazon shareholders, Bezos wrote:

"One area where I think we are especially distinctive is failure. I believe we are the best place in the world to fail (we have plenty of practice!), and failure and invention are inseparable twins. To invent you have to experiment, and if you know in advance that it's going to work, it's not an experiment."

In 2000, Bezos launched an aerospace company, Blue Origin, with the vision of "enabling a future where millions of people are living and working in space for the benefit of Earth."

Bezos' leadership style is best described as complicated, but it gets results.

Construction was scheduled to be completed in November 2019 but there were some delays and we were finally finished in February 2020. On the day it opened, the space was booked solid for months. The first act to use the studio was the rock band Tame Impala. And then the pandemic shutdown happened. All those back-to-back bookings disappeared.

But then they started coming back. Even though the hotels and shows in Vegas were still shuttered, the artists needed a place to work. And we just happened to have the type of space they needed. The Uber Eats Super Bowl commercial was shot in our studio. An Aflac commercial has been shot there. Bands like The Killers and artists like Lindsey Stirling have shot music videos in our facility. Other acts, including John Legend and the Backstreet Boys, have used it as a place to prep for tours.

It was a $1 million calculated risk driven by my intuition and it paid off.

Sometimes intuition is what drives you to seek a solution—you know there's an answer, but you don't know what it is. With the expansion of our Las Vegas warehouse/studio, we needed additional parking. My intuition told me not to simply accept and learn to live with the problem.

There was a vacant parcel of land adjacent to our property that had been acquired by eminent domain when the big interchange of I-15 and I-215 was built about twenty years ago. The parcel wasn't large enough to put a building on, but it was perfect for us to solve our need for parking.

When I approached the Clark County Department of Aviation, which owned the property, about acquiring it, they told me I had two options: wait for the property to come up for auction or find out who the land had been taken from and try to get the reversionary rights. It took some digging, but we found the previous owner of the land. Fortunately, he was still alive and happy to make a deal for the reversionary rights. That meant I was able to reclaim the land, get it permitted, and solve my parking issue.

Recently I watched my teenage son demonstrate some amazing intuition. He bought a non-fungible token (NFT) for $700 and sold it a few hours later for $25,000 (that's not a typo—he bought for seven hundred and sold for twenty-five thousand). I don't understand how the value of NFTs is created, but he does, and I'm cheering him on.

Great leaders develop and use their intuition. Of course they get as much information as they can about whatever they're dealing with, but they trust their intuition to fill in the blanks.

Intuition works best when you know yourself, when you know how to pay attention to those feelings like that "I can't explain it but" sense that's telling you to go or that little twinge in your gut that's telling you to stop. I can't always articulate it to others, but I know when my intuition is working and I've learned how to listen to it.

WHEN THERE'S NO PERFECT OPTION

Some life and business decisions are easy. If it's unethical or illegal, we don't do it. Period. If we've had a performance failure, we do whatever it takes to make it right, even if it means losing money. End of discussion.

But not all decisions are that simple or clear. Sometimes there are no good options and it's not a case of the best choice, it's a case of the least bad choice or the lesser of the evils. Not every decision is going to be good for everybody. We saw this over and over during the pandemic, especially when it came to keeping employees when we didn't have any work for them to do. Companies that tried to do that eventually ran out of money and some had to shut down. It was hard to terminate people who served our company well for years, but we didn't have a choice when their positions were no longer required, and we couldn't reassign them. There will be situations where, if you try to save everyone, you could end up saving no one and destroying the business. So you make the least bad choice by letting some people go and preserving the company. You have to make decisions that are ultimately in the best interests of the organization, and those decisions may not always be for the benefit of individuals.

SOMETIMES YOU'RE WRONG

Not all of your decisions will be right. Maybe you didn't have enough information. Maybe you just made an error in judgment. Whatever the reason, when you make the wrong decision, you still have to own it. You take responsibility for your decisions, whatever the outcome. That, more than any other single thing, will earn you the respect and loyalty of your team.

Great leaders are respected but not feared. Fear of the leader will destroy an organization from the inside.

Chapter Five

Building a Team

W hen your company is small and it's just you and maybe a few other people, you make all the decisions. You also do most of the work. As you grow, you need to build a team of people who share the work and take on leadership responsibilities. If you try to do it all on your own, you'll never be able to scale your business. If you want to grow your business, survive crises, and provide opportunities for the employees you have, you need to identify people with leadership potential to help you.

The concept of building a leadership team is simple: Surround yourself with people who are smarter than you and have skills in areas that complement yours.

Actually doing it can be a challenge. Entrepreneurs often find it difficult to relinquish control and delegate. They may enjoy doing the work of the business more than they do running the business, which is probably the most common reason small businesses fail to grow. And it's human nature to want to spend time with people we like—and we typically like people whose personalities are similar to ours. But growing a company means building a team of people who aren't just like you and who can do things you can't. As the leader, you have to be in charge of the big picture. You're the visionary and troubleshooter. You must delegate and not get bogged down in jobs other people can do.

I wouldn't trade the years I spent doing the work necessary to stage shows. Setting up gear, running cables, operating equipment— all of that and more taught me what I needed to know to grow ETP into the industry leader it is today. But I knew that to grow the company, there came a point when I had to stop doing those things, when I could no longer work as part of the crew. I found good people to work in the business while I worked on growing it.

Leaders have to recognize and appreciate the importance of the supporting players on their team. It's a concept that's easy to see in team sports. Many teams have one or two star players, but those stars are very much supported by the rest of the team and they couldn't be stars without the team. As the leader, you may be the star, but without the team, you can't perform.

Be intentional about building your team. Start with an honest understanding of who you are and what makes you tick. Know what you need and want. Then work to build a team with a diverse set of skills, experience, and styles. Great leadership teams grow by having people who come to the team with different perspectives. We don't need another Les Goldberg at ETP. We have one; that's enough. (And I'm sure there are some people on our team who would tell you that's more than enough.) We need people who know things I don't know, who have skills I don't have, and who will honestly share their experience and knowledge. They have to be compatible because they need to work together, but they shouldn't be homogenous. A team with people who are all mirror images of one another will collapse. I've seen it happen in other organizations many times.

Your leadership team needs to operate on commitment, not consensus. Consensus means that everybody agrees. If you've got ten people on your leadership team who always agree with one another, you don't need nine of them. You want people who have strong opinions and are willing to go to bat for what they believe. When a team operates on commitment to the organization, they may disagree, but they have internal alignment, they are results oriented, and they take ownership of what they do.

Even though you want people who complement each other and bring diverse skills to the table, there are things you want them to have in common. Some things I look for include:

Integrity. This is a no-brainer. I want people whose honesty and ethics are above reproach. It's how I operate and it's what I expect from everyone in the ETP organization. The end never justifies the means if the means are unethical.

Communication skills. In addition to whatever technical skills they have, members of my leadership team have to be good communicators. They must be good listeners as well as able to express themselves clearly.

Good sounding boards. They need to be able to listen to ideas and contribute to a collective evaluation so we can decide how to move forward.

High energy and the ability to get things done. Some people talk a good case but don't actually get things done. I want people who not only have great ideas but who can implement them and get results.

Growth potential. The people on my leadership team demonstrate a desire to grow as individuals and as part of the team. They're always looking for ways to improve, to develop their skills and expand their abilities. And they learn from each other because they know that as they become stronger individually the team becomes stronger collectively.

A desire to be part of the team. This is key—they must want to be on the team. They have to share a commitment to the company's mission and purpose.

Trust your team

Effective leadership requires a high level of trust. Your team has to trust you and you have to trust that they will perform to the expectations you've developed.

Leaders who don't trust their teams will never be successful. Teams who don't trust their leaders will never be able to reach their

Leadership in Action: Walt Disney

The creative, innovative, and complex Walt Disney started from scratch to build his name into one of the most recognized global brands. In the early days, he was a driven, charismatic man who was an inspiration to all his employees. As the company grew, Disney's authoritarian leadership style emerged.

Disney wasn't a born leader; he acquired his skills over time. He learned how to put people at ease and was an excellent communicator.

One of Disney's trademark leadership characteristics was that he did not impose rigid job descriptions. He knew that most people have a range of talents, skills, and interests, and he didn't pigeonhole people.

Disney had a high tolerance for risk and wasn't afraid of failure. He was a confident decision-maker who never hesitated once a decision was made. He was curious, always learning and exploring, always trying new things.

While he had a good relationship with his workers, he was also known for firing people who disagreed with him on the spot. He wasn't interested in conflict resolution. It wasn't that he was unfair or didn't care, but he wanted to do things his way. Even so, he learned from his mistakes and didn't blame others. And he remained humble, saying, "I only hope that we never lose sight of one thing—that it all started with a mouse."

full potential. But when there's trust, the possibilities are endless.

So how do you create trust?

- Do the simple things well and consistently.
- Keep your word.
- Care for the people you lead and show it.
- Take responsibility when things go wrong and give credit to others when things go right.
- Don't play favorites.
- Share information.

The best leaders don't hoard information, they share as much as possible—even when things aren't going well. Poor leaders avoid straightforward discussions and creative brainstorming. They like the sense of exclusivity they feel when they know things others don't. And while confidentiality is certainly important for some things, failing to pass on important information promptly, consistently, and accurately can create mistrust and limit everyone's ability to perform at their best.

I have a "no yes-person" policy not only for my leadership team, but throughout the company. I don't want anyone agreeing with me just because I'm the boss; I want honest opinions and innovative ideas shared in an atmosphere of respect and courtesy. Everyone on our leadership team knows they can let their guard down and no one is going to sling arrows at them. They know they can disagree and express opinions that may be unpopular because we welcome diversity of thought.

LEADERSHIP TEAMS ARE ALWAYS EVOLVING

The larger your organization, the more leadership teams you'll have. We have the executive team at the top of ETP, but then each company, each division, each operating entity has its own teams.

Your teams will change as your needs change. As the company grows, you'll need new skills and perspectives. You may need to replace people who leave—because no matter how great of an employer you are, people will leave. Some will retire, some will leave for other opportunities, and occasionally some will die. As a leader, you need to recognize this reality and be prepared to mitigate the impact of turnover on your organization.

When the country began to reopen as the COVID-19 pandemic eased in the spring of 2021, we saw a higher-than-normal quit rate among American workers that continued into 2022 and became known as the Great Resignation. (Some people are now calling it the Great Regret, but that's a discussion for another time.) As job openings increased and the unemployment rate decreased, a record number of Americans decided it was a good time to leave their employers. We weren't immune; we saw a definite uptick in departures.

No matter how hard or easy it will be to find the right replacement, when people are ready to leave, let them go. You can offer them all kinds of incentives to stay and they might stick around for a while, but you've only delayed the inevitable because they'll eventually leave. Sometimes people just want a change. They want a new opportunity. And you don't want anyone in your company who doesn't want to be there.

Sometimes you'll get the wrong person in the job, either because of a bad hire or a promotion error. Either way, it's an expensive mistake you have to accept and deal with. Once you realize it, you must take swift action. Having someone who doesn't fit is worse than not having anyone at all.

We have a comprehensive screening process for new hires but occasionally we get surprised. Once we hired a guy for a key leadership position. He made it through our vetting process, and we thought we'd made a good choice. He came in and on day one wanted to turn everything upside down. He thought he knew a better way to do everything, but his ideas weren't good, they didn't fit our culture, and they weren't going to work. He lasted less than a week.

Remember, if someone isn't right for the company, the company isn't right for them. Don't let them stay in a place that isn't good for them. Help them to move on where they'll be happier, more fulfilled, and more productive.

INVEST IN YOUR PEOPLE

In the past, we never had trouble attracting good people, but getting the great talent our clients expect us to have is much tougher now. Though I've always believed in investing in our people with things like training, a great work environment, and benefits, what was a bonus years ago is essential now.

As it does in just about every area of your business, the law of supply and demand has a serious impact on staffing. When the demand for good people exceeds the supply, the good people can be more selective about where they work. While a competitive compensation and benefit package is important, you have to do more than that to get the people you need. We give our people opportunities to learn and grow, to try different career tracks. We train them. We let them try working in various departments to see what they like best.

Years ago, our leadership team recognized the importance of training and development not only for everyone in our company, but for the industry in general. Though many companies, including ours, encouraged training and mentoring by the more experienced, skilled workers, we realized the benefit would be exponentially greater if the training was done a systematic, structured way. We created a learning center we call CoIL, which stands for Continuous Improvement and Learning. We've developed partnerships with universities around the world to deliver hands-on learning opportunities in entertainment technology that helps students jumpstart a career in the field.

Through CoIL, we offer courses in leadership development and productivity, technical training, soft skills coaching, and more, along
with apprenticeships; internships; and networking events. Even
when we were forced to make cuts during the pandemic, we didn't
cut CoIL—that's how important this program is.

Leadership in Action: Bill Gates

For years, Bill Gates has been known as one of the world's
wealthiest people. His story as a Harvard drop-out who co-founded
Microsoft Corporation and has since pursued many business and phil-
anthropic endeavors is well-known. But it took more than an interest
in technology for Gates to become a billionaire at the age of 31—it
took leadership.

Gates is a passionate and resilient leader who sees learning as
a lifelong process. He's not complacent; he's high energy and doesn't
settle for the status quo.

Using a transformational leadership style, he empowers his team
members, practicing intellectual stimulation to encourage them to
identify and solve problems creatively. He believes in individualized
consideration, which is when leaders pay special attention to each
individual's needs and recognize their achievements.

Gates has said that learning to delegate better is one of the many
lessons he's learned about leadership. In particular, he had to learn to
delegate his weaknesses to other people's strengths.

Of course, no one is perfect. Gates sometimes crosses that fine
line between confidence and arrogance. He has a reputation of being uncomfortable with conflict and avoiding issues that need to be
confronted. His social and political views are mixed, and just about
everyone can find things to love and hate about him.

Years ago, Gates said, "As we look ahead into the next century,
leaders will be those who empower others." He was—and still is—right
about that.

Think about it like this: You want to make a tomato and brie salad so you head to the grocery store and buy the best looking beefsteak tomato, and you go home and make a great salad. But what if the store doesn't have any tomatoes? If you had planted your own tomatoes, if you had watered and fertilized them, and nurtured them until they grew and ripened, it wouldn't matter what the store had in stock. That's what we do with our people. We have programs that take them from seedlings (people who want to learn our business) to full-grown plants that are producing fruit (trained and skilled members of our team). It's how we live out our commitment to transmit knowledge to future generations.

When it comes to people and staffing, your job as a leader is to find good raw material and develop them. If they're inexperienced, train them. If they're experienced, give them an opportunity to hone their skills and get better.

Remember that the beautiful diamonds you see in jewelry don't come out of the ground looking like that. After they're mined, they're polished and cut before they become beautiful pieces of art.

It's important for a company to invest in its people—all of them, at every level, but especially the leadership team. You do that by providing coaching, mentoring, and training, which I'll discuss further in Chapter 8.

HUMAN ERROR HAPPENS

I have tremendous respect for someone who comes to me and says, "I made a decision, I took this action, and it turned out to be wrong. I accept responsibility and here's what I plan to do."

Sometimes an idea that seemed good on paper doesn't work out in reality. Sometimes a ball gets dropped. Those things are going to happen, and when they do, I need to know about it—and I need to know the truth.

Even the best, the sharpest, most talented, highest skilled people will make mistakes, and they must be held accountable when they do. Nobody ever gets so high up in an organization that they can't learn from their mistakes. I like to sit down with the person

Leadership in Action: Albert Einstein

Albert Einstein is widely acknowledged to be one of the greatest physicists of all time, best known for developing the theory of relativity.

Einstein's strongest leadership skill was inquisitiveness. He said, "The important thing is to not stop questioning." Like all great leaders, he wasn't satisfied with the way things are because he knew they could be better.

Einstein learned to use analogies to simplify complexity and communicate his groundbreaking theories to common people. He said, "To simplify the concept of relativity, I always use the following example: if you sit with a girl on a garden bench and the moon is shining, then for you the hour will be a minute. However, if you sit on a hot stove, the minute will be an hour."

Einstein was also willing to admit when he was wrong. When he was in school and in the early days of his career, he had little regard for the field of mathematics. He later realized the importance and creativity of the field while working on his theory of relativity.

He was tenacious, known for his perseverance. He said, "It's not that I'm so smart, it's just that I stay with problems longer."

He also had a tremendous imagination, which he thought was more important than knowledge. To make children intelligent, Einstein recommended reading them fairy tales. And to make them more intelligent, he said, read them more fairy tales.

Finally, he thought the best solutions were the simple ones. He said, "Any intelligent fool can make things bigger, more complex. It takes a touch of genius, and a lot of courage, to move in the opposite direction."

who was responsible for a problem and reflect on what happened. I have a simple series of questions: What went wrong? How did we get here? What have we learned? What are we going to do to make sure it doesn't happen again? And then I trust them to let the experience make them better.

EQUAL ACCESSIBILITY

Great leaders are approachable and able to take bad news without shooting the messenger. They know that waiting isn't going to make bad news better—a problem is only going to get worse if you delay dealing with it, so they create a culture where people aren't afraid to approach them, to make suggestions, and to be honest about what's really going on. My leadership team even manages to have a little fun with it. There's one member of the team who, when she has bad news, always starts with, "Mr. Goldberg," and I know I'm probably not going to like what she says next. But I also know I need to hear it.

Being approachable and accessible is a two-way street. One of the things I tell everyone who comes to work for our company on the first day I meet them is this: "I want you to know that if I need you in the middle of the night, I will call you. If it takes waking you up at two in the morning to save a show, that's what we do. And you can call me, too." I want to set expectations. I want them to know that if they need me, I'm here for them, but if I need them, I'm calling with no apologies.

Have I been taken up on this? Many times. Once my phone rang at one o'clock in the morning. It was the leader of a crew that was setting up a pharmaceutical show in Arizona. The manufacturer of a projector we were using had upgraded the software and the upgrade had disabled some of the features we used, but we weren't told about it. Over the next few hours, I was on the phone with various people in our company and the manufacturer in Europe. By four o'clock in the morning, I knew we had a major problem. We ended up taking down eighteen projectors that were in the air and replacing them with equipment we had scrambled to locate and get shipped in from the west coast. It was classic business triage on the fly. A bunch of us lost some sleep, but we were able to make the show happen as planned and keep the customer happy. That wouldn't have been the case if any of the calls that got made in the middle of the night had waited until morning.

We also learned a lesson, which was to always do a full check on equipment that's had software upgrades to make sure all the features are working.

I do this because we are a team and no one in our organization works in isolation. I don't expect anyone to do anything I'm not willing to do myself, but I do expect people to give their best and I'll do whatever it takes to help them do that.

CHAPTER SIX

RISKS, REWARDS, AND MONEY

Life is one enormous risk. Driving to work involves risk. Walking up and down stairs involves risk. When you order a meal in a restaurant, you're taking a risk that the food was prepared properly and won't make you sick. Those are just some of the things we do every day without thinking of the risk involved.

We give more thought to things with a greater level of risk, a level that could lead to crises—potentially dangerous sports, serious surgeries, and venturing into high-crime areas. Certainly a trip into space on Sir Richard Branson's Virgin Galactic rocket plane or Jeff Bezos' Blue Origin rocket is a bigger risk than I want to take. Nik Wallenda is known for risking his life when he performed untethered tightrope walks over the Grand Canyon and Niagara Falls. We didn't work with him on those stunts, but we've worked with him a few times at other events. He gets paid a lot of money for the stunts he does. Is the risk worth the reward? For him, apparently so. For me, not so much.

Beyond physical risk is a wide range of emotional, business, and financial risks that we face regularly. Some of those risks make us fearful; others generate a sense of excitement and opportunity. No two people deal with risk in the exact same way.

When it comes to risk, some people are super-liberal, they're thrill-seekers, they're adrenaline junkies. They take risks for the sake of taking risks. At the other end of the spectrum are the people who are super-conservative who don't take any risks. They play it safe; they'd live in a bubble if they could. But they're not really living because they're so afraid to do anything. And then there are the billions of people on the planet who fall in between those two extremes.

We all have our own level of risk tolerance that's formed by a variety of influences. What one person sees as an exciting adventure, another might see as an unacceptable degree of risk. But great rewards usually have great risk. We value and admire people who have had big dreams, taken great risks, and been successful. And even though what we do in our day-to-day lives rarely has the excitement or visibility of a space flight or a high wire walk over a volcano, it still has plenty of risk.

TAKE CALCULATED NOT IRRESPONSIBLE RISKS

Are you willing to risk $1,000 in a poker game? If you're a millionaire and you enjoy playing cards, you might be. If that's more than a week's salary and losing could mean not making your rent or mortgage payment, probably not.

When it comes to taking risks, we need to know and understand our comfort zones. In this context, I'm not talking about the comfort zones you hear personal development gurus talk about, such as if you tend to be shy, get out of your comfort zone by walking up to a stranger and introducing yourself. I'm talking about how much you're willing to lose and what other parameters influence you. My risk-related comfort zone is defined by how much control I have over the situation and how much I'm willing to lose.

I take a lot of what some people consider high-stakes business risks, but they're calculated risks. The outcome isn't guaranteed but I've done everything in my power to make sure the odds are in my favor, and I have a strong degree of control over the outcome. I'm not willing to take risks just for the thrill of it.

Once I was in a casino with a friend who decided we were going to play blackjack, and he asked, "Are you good with a $500 table or a $1,000 table?" I've never bet $1,000 on anything in a casino. I'm not a big gambler; I don't find casino games entertaining. I also know that everything in a casino is weighted in favor of the house. Even though I could afford the higher stakes tables, my response was, "I'm more comfortable with a $100 table."

By the time we were finished, I had won $1,800 and he lost $10,000, but that's not the point. Could we both afford to risk thousands of dollars gambling? Yes. My friend's loss was no big deal to him financially—although it probably did some damage to his ego. Do we find gambling entertaining and stimulating? My friend does, and he enjoys going to casinos to gamble; I don't, so even though I'm often in casinos in the course of my business, I rarely gamble.

Some of the risks I enjoy taking are ones that have the potential to grow my company. The people on my leadership team could probably spend hours telling stories of times when I've taken huge risks, such as buying leading edge equipment when we didn't know if our customers would use it or building new facilities without a clearly identified market for them. But I don't do those things on a whim; even though there are times when it might seem like I've gone crazy, I'm very calculated. I've thought things through and I know what I'm doing.

While we tend to think primarily about financial risk when we're thinking of business, there are plenty of other areas of risk we need to consider. That's why the global insurance industry is worth more than $6 trillion. In fact, studying how insurance works is a great way to teach yourself how to assess risk and understand your own risk tolerance.

There's a lot of risk in the people gathering business. It's fraught with potential points of failure, from transportation to installation and the equipment itself. Events require a tremendous amount of equipment, and each piece of equipment has an element of risk. When we did a show called Executive Focus International, former President George H. W. Bush and former Secretary of State Colin Powell were featured speakers. As Bush walked to the stage, he went up to the crew and said, "Okay, boys, let's not screw this one up." (We didn't.) As Powell was making his way to the stage, he looked at all the backstage equipment and said, "We fought wars with less

Leadership in Action: Sitting Bull

As the leader of the Sioux and supreme chief of all tribes, Sitting Bull consistently demonstrated the essential ability to develop himself and others. He was caring and generous with his followers, and embodied tribe values, making him the perfect choice as leader.

At the Battle of Little Bighorn, Sitting Bull taught a lesson today's leaders should heed: Know and respect your opponent (competition) and be accurate in evaluating their strength.

Sitting Bull was a leader who kept his word and couldn't be corrupted. He was able to mobilize his forces though his own commitment and integrity. He shared power with others to work toward a common vision and developed young warriors into the leaders he knew they could become. He was flexible and adapted to changing circumstances. From Sitting Bull, we can learn that true leadership is built on authenticity backed by achievement.

Perhaps the essence of Sitting Bull as a leader was his willingness to step forward and take responsibility for himself, his followers, and future generations. One of his most famous quotes is: "Let us put our minds together and see what life we can make for our children."

amount of gear than this."

Sometimes when people ask me what we do, I say that we put big, heavy things over people's heads—and we don't want any of those things to fall. We know how to install the equipment securely and we have a series of safety redundancy procedures we follow. Beyond that, there's always the risk that the equipment won't function properly or that it won't arrive at the event in time. There's the risk of human error at any step of the process. And then there are the external risks such as pandemics, cyberattacks, and geopolitical threats.

Effective leaders know their own risk tolerance and they have a clear picture of which risks pose the greatest threat to them personally as well as to the company. They make risk management and mitigation a routine function of the leadership team. Though that sounds complicated, it really comes down to applying a simple policy when it comes to risk: Be responsible by never risking more than you are willing to lose and don't take big risks when you don't have control of the outcome.

BANKING AND FINANCE

In addition to being passionate about their businesses, great leaders have a solid understanding of business finance and they know how to deal with banks, lenders, and investors. You can hire accountants and advisors, but when the buck stops with you, you need to be able to make an informed decision. Knowing how to deal with financial institutions is a requirement for entrepreneurs and leaders.

A lot of what I know about banks I learned the hard way through a combination of good choices, mistakes, and experience.

Way back in LMG's early days, when I was signing the paperwork for one of my first business loans, I asked my banker, Paul, "What does all this mean?"

He said, "If you don't pay the bank, bad things happen."

I got the message.

You'll find the financial world easier to navigate if you know how it works before you're in the middle of it. I'm going to give you a crash course here, but I also recommend that you spend some time educating yourself further.

Traditionally, banks loan money and provide financial products like checking accounts, savings accounts, safe deposit boxes, and some investment services. They make their money on loan interest and service fees. They're highly regulated and very anti-risk. You've probably heard people say that banks only want to lend money to people who don't need it. That's not far from reality—banks only want to lend money to people when they're sure they'll get paid back. Yet most businesses depend on having substantial lines of credit available to operate. It's an interesting cycle—companies need to borrow money to make money to pay back the money they've borrowed so they can qualify to borrow more money.

Banks typically make their loans on one of two principles: the value of the borrower's assets or the borrower's profitability. A real estate mortgage is the classic example of an asset loan—the bank lends you money based on the value of the property you want to buy or build, and it's a simple formula. Borrowing on profitability is a little more complicated and banks have different ways of calculating what they'll lend you based on your company's performance.

Banks have what they call relationship managers who are essentially salespeople. They'll call you up to see how you're doing, they'll come to your office to handle your transactions. If you need a loan, they put the package together and take it to the credit committee with a recommendation. They'll do all kinds of things for you as long as the bank is making money from your accounts and you conform to all their criteria.

When times are good, the traditional banking model works fine for everyone. When the economy gets tight or when there's a downturn in business, banks start looking for ways to get rid of customers that they believe have become high-risk. If you fall into that category—as so many industries did during the COVID pandemic—you've got a serious problem.

How banks dealt with the pandemic

To tell this story so you can truly appreciate it, I would name the banks and bankers involved. However, my attorney has advised me that doing so could put me at risk of being sued, even though everything I'm going to tell you is true. I donate all the money I receive from my books to St. Jude Children's Research Hospital and I don't want to put myself in a position of having to spend any of those funds defending a lawsuit. So I'm not naming the banks or bankers, but the banks are among the largest in the U.S., and if you really want to know who they are, you can probably figure it out with just a little research. With that disclaimer, here's the story:

When we started Entertainment Technology Partners, we approached six banks. Four of them made offers immediately because they liked our story and thought we were low risk. One declined. At the last minute, Bank A swooped in, offered us more than what we were asking for, and won the deal. We launched ETP in 2014 and it was a success out of the gate. The business grew and in 2018, our banker called and told us that because we were doing so well, they wanted to increase our line of credit. Well, of course! When the good times are rolling, banks love you. And times were good. Everybody was making money—we were happy, the bank was happy. It stayed that way through 2019, which was a record year for revenue and profit.

Fast forward to 2020. The year got off to a great start, but in March, the whole world changed. COVID-19 shut down the US

Leadership in Action: Warren Buffett

One of the world's wealthiest people, Warren Buffett is often referred to as the "oracle" or "sage" of Omaha. In his 2015 letter to Berkshire Hathaway shareholders, he wrote: "Much of what you become in life depends on whom you choose to admire and copy." In other words, copy the best.

As a leader, Buffett is a confident visionary. He's optimistic, adaptive, a great mentor and deep thinker. He appreciates the efforts of his employees and associates, and he's very good at saying no. He said, "The difference between successful people and really successful people is that really successful people say 'no' to almost everything." He also says that successful businesspeople know how to take calculated risks and accept the consequences of their decisions.

Buffett attributes his incredible success largely to hiring the right people and says integrity counts most when assessing job candidates. One of Buffett's most popular quotes is:

"We look for three things when we hire people. We look for intelligence, we look for initiative or energy, and we look for integrity. And if they don't have the latter, the first two will kill you, because if you're going to get someone without integrity, you want them lazy and dumb. You don't want them smart and energetic."

Buffett's letters to shareholders reveal as much about him as they do about Berkshire Hathaway. One thing he does in those letters is to mention people by name when he recognizes them for their contributions to the company.

He's known for being humble and kind. He lives modestly and is one of the world's most generous philanthropists. In his Giving Pledge letter, he wrote: "More than 99% of my wealth will go to philanthropy during my lifetime or at death. ... [that wealth] can have a huge effect on the health and welfare of others. That reality sets an obvious course for me and my family: Keep all we can conceivably need and distribute the rest to society, for its needs."

economy. While industries deemed essential continued to function, those considered non-essential struggled. Unfortunately, the people gathering industry was considered non-essential and that made it difficult for us to function at all, much less operate at the levels of profitability we had routinely enjoyed.

To understand the magnitude of this, consider that in its 50-plus-year history, Walt Disney World in Orlando has had only nine unscheduled closures. Seven of those were for a partial day or up to two days because of hurricanes. One was for one day after the September 11 attacks. And then COVID-19 hit in 2020, and the resort's theme parks closed for almost four months from March 15 until July 11, when they began reopening with limited capacity.

When shutdowns began in March of 2020, our bank immediately went into self-preservation mode. Its primary goal was to reduce its own exposure, even though that meant taking on the role of grim reaper with many of its customers, including us.

Of course, we were in self-preservation mode, too. When live gatherings shut down, we responded by shifting that portion of our business to virtual events. But we couldn't do it overnight. Still, even though times were tough, we were figuring it out.

I knew a lot of people who were having trouble with their banks at the time. We were all in unknown territory and the banks were understandably trying to mitigate their risk. Some people suggested that I max out our line of credit and put that cash in a different bank because the more you owe a bank, the more leverage you have. I didn't do that because I didn't think it was the responsible thing to do. But I want to share what happened so you can learn from my experience.

Banks typically look at the world through the viewpoint of quarters. They rely on a calculation known as trailing twelve months (TTM) to evaluate a company's financial health and determine if it is meeting its loan covenants. Based on the economy and what had happened to our industry during the early days of the pandemic, our TTM did not meet our covenants (the terms of our line of credit) in the second quarter of 2020. The reason was simple: it took us and our customers some time to make the shift from in-person gatherings to online events. We were still doing events; we just weren't shipping equipment all over the world because online events didn't require that type of gear.

In July, Bank A notified us that our credit line was being substantially reduced—and for this reduction, we had the privilege of paying hefty loan fees. We understood and agreed to it for two primary reasons: first, we didn't have much choice, and second, we were focused on doing whatever was necessary to keep the company going, to restore the business lost during the pandemic, and to gain new market shares. Even though things were working, our third quarter numbers did not meet our covenants again and Bank A put on the full court press. They assigned a team of people to our account, demanded that our CFO produce documents and provide information that took a significant amount of time to research and compile. Next came all kinds of crazy additional requirements for collateral asset evaluations and reporting. They were essentially making our CFO spin in circles. It was so painful and stressful—it was like their job was to torture us.

Still, I believed the bank going to do the right thing. After all, we'd been with them for almost seven years as good clients. By the end of 2020, we had successfully staged more than one thousand virtual events and business was growing again—and I got a call from the bank saying they were lowering our line of credit again and I had to put $5 million of my own capital into the company. It was a big ask and I wasn't happy about it. But I knew people who were facing similar demands from their banks and weren't able to meet them. Some of those businesses were forced to close, some were forced into bankruptcy, and other capitulated to their banks' demands and paid exorbitant fees they would never have been charged under normal circumstances.

Then on April 8, 2021, Bank A notified us of an urgent meeting on April 9 but didn't tell us what it was about. I was scheduled to be out of town, but I changed my plans so I could attend. In that meeting, they told us they had cut our credit line again. In the middle of

Leadership in Action: Andrew Carnegie

Scottish-American industrialist and philanthropist Andrew Carnegie led the expansion of the American steel industry in the late nineteenth century and became one of the richest Americans in history.

Carnegie's family emigrated to the United States when he was thirteen. Even at that age, he was industrious, working first in a cotton mill, then as a telegraph operator, then for the Pennsylvania Railroad. His keen eye for opportunity helped him amass business interests in iron works, steamers on the Great Lakes, railroads, and oil wells by the age of thirty.

Self-educated and a voracious reader, one of Carnegie's many philanthropies was gifts of free public library buildings. He believed that wealthy people had a responsibility to spend their money to benefit the greater good.

The "Andrew Carnegie Dictum" was:

To spend the first third of one's life getting all the education one can.

To spend the next third making all the money one can.

To spend the last third giving it all away for worthwhile causes.

Carnegie pledged to give away all his money before he died. While he didn't quite succeed (he had about $30 million at his death, which was given to foundations, charities, and pensioners), he left an amazing legacy of civic leadership.

One of Carnegie's best-known quotes is: "No man will make a great leader who wants to do it all himself or get all the credit for doing it."

the night on April 8, without any notice, they cut our already-reduced credit line in half. At that point, our credit line was twenty percent of what it had been in March 2020.

The bank gave us a letter explaining that they thought we were going to lose money for the rest of 2021 which would keep us out of compliance, so they were reducing our credit line. They weren't willing to negotiate or even listen to what we were doing. And they asked me to put another $5 million of my own money into the business.

After that call, I have never talked to any of the bankers who were in that meeting again.

Not only did we *not* lose money in 2021, we ended the year with a substantial profit. I sometimes wonder how much more we could have made if the bank had worked *with* us instead of *against* us.

I understand that banks need to protect their interests, manage their risks, and meet a variety of regulatory requirements in their lending practices. I also know that in challenging times, some banks will do their best to get rid of all their customers that are in what they think are high-risk industries, even the customers in those industries that are doing well. We saw that over and over during the pandemic—companies that suffered and sometimes failed completely because they couldn't get the credit they needed to get them through the shutdown until they could resume normal operations. It's unfortunate that as the banks do short-sighted things to protect themselves, they can harm their customers.

I don't think I'm unusual in that I need a bank that's going to work with me, that's going to take the time to get to know me, that will build a relationship with me based on mutual trust and respect, and that wants to see my company succeed. So when Bank A's demands became unreasonable and almost impossible to meet, I went shopping for a new bank.

Within 30 days, I found Synovus, a bank based in Columbus, Georgia. I personally met with Kevin Blair, the bank's president and

CEO, as well as the credit team. I explained our business, how we operate, what we had done and were doing to survive the pandemic and continue to grow. They decided we were a good risk, and I can't speak highly enough about how great they are to work with.

I lost a lot of sleep while we were going through this process of Bank A cutting our credit line and making arbitrary demands, but it was my job as the leader to deal with this challenge. I knew we could come up with a plan and find a bank that believed in us. It just took the iron will I talked about in Chapter 3.

Bank A is not the only bank we had issues with during the crazy days of the pandemic. We had a loan on one of our facilities with Bank B. Like Bank A, Bank B was targeting our industry. Because we were in the people gathering business, they put us into something called the ARG, which stands for asset recovery group. The people who work in a bank's ARG are financially incentivized to get rid of customers without the bank losing money, and they do everything they can to achieve that goal. This was a very short-sighted approach on Bank B's part because we were dealing with a real estate loan that had over fifty percent equity. They kept making unreasonable requests; we kept making our payments.

All loans have what's known as a MAC clause, which essentially says that if your business has a material adverse change, they can declare you out of compliance and call the loan. The ARG ordered an unnecessary appraisal on our Las Vegas warehouse/studio and, if the value had declined substantially, they could have invoked the MAC clause. But the value had increased by $4 million, giving us sixty-five percent equity, which is almost unheard of in commercial real estate. Even with that, Bank B continued to operate in a way that seemed like their mission was to make my life miserable. They were trying to make it so difficult to work with them that I would take my business elsewhere. And they succeeded. I finally had enough and refinanced that property with another bank.

There were times during this process that I thought of that banker who told me, "If you don't pay the bank, bad things happen." Well, sometimes even if you do pay the bank, bad things can happen. If you're not in alignment with your bank and the bank decides that they don't want your business anymore, they will do everything they can to make your life miserable and get you out of the bank.

This banking issue was a crisis within a crisis for us. It was challenging enough to be dealing with a worldwide pandemic that had turned our industry upside down, but it was even worse to be doing it without the financial partners we'd come to depend on. But we survived, we found a new bank, and I learned some valuable lessons about how important it is to have strong banking relationships at the highest levels so you can not only do well in good times but also survive in bad times.

CHAPTER SEVEN

LEADING THROUGH CRISES

Crises come in a variety of sizes and shapes. A business crisis could be a major product or service failure, the departure or death of a key person, a physical disaster that damages your facility, a cyberattack, theft, pandemic—the list is endless. The crisis might happen and be resolved in a day, or it could take weeks, months, or even years. The degree of damage a crisis inflicts and how well you survive it depends largely on the effectiveness of your leadership team.

We talked about the importance of leadership teams in Chapter 5, but let me stress that having a strong leadership team is essential when a crisis hits. You need those tested, proven advisors ready to address the issue, discuss a variety of viewpoints, make decisions, and take action.

Maybe you had an employee suffer a serious on-the-job injury. You need to deal with the injured individual and provide support to their family. You also need to deal with the co-workers who may have witnessed the incident, giving them whatever assistance they need. If the situation is going to affect a customer, you must address that promptly. And while you're doing all of this, you need to keep the company running.

Or let's say you're the victim of a ransomware attack, which is when hackers gain access to your IT systems, lock them down, and attempt to extort money from you in exchange for restoring your access to your data. It's like having an invisible person holding a gun to your head. This happened to us years ago and since then we've done everything we can to prevent it from happening again. We have the best possible security and enough redundancies so we can continue to function if something happens. We regularly evaluate and update our systems. No company is totally invulnerable but it's critical to have strong systems to protect your data.

When you're dealing with a crisis, no matter what it is, you have to keep your purpose and mission in mind. When you're clear on what they are, you can keep communicating them during the crisis, and that will help you stay focused on what you need to do to manage the crisis and get back to normal.

In our industry, crises are often related to transportation. When you're moving people and equipment around the world for events as we do, there are plenty of opportunities for things to go wrong and we have to be ready to respond quickly when they do. Years ago, we were doing a pharmaceutical meeting in Puerto Rico. Our equipment was scheduled to be delivered on Saturday morning for a show that was to begin Monday. The shipping company dropped the ball and didn't show up with our equipment. By the time we heard about the situation at our headquarters in Orlando, it was early evening on Saturday. I tracked down our shipping company contact in Puerto Rico. The representative was out on a fishing boat with his son, and all he had to say was sorry, he couldn't help us, and the container would be delivered sometime on Monday.

That was too late. The client's event was starting on Monday and they needed to rehearse on Sunday. So we figured out what we needed to get us through rehearsals, packed everything in forty-six road cases that were small enough to go on a passenger plane as baggage, and rushed them to the airport in time for the last flight on Saturday. Our crew had time to set things up on Sunday so we could do rehearsals and be ready for the meeting to begin Monday. We lost some sleep and we spent a lot of money on extra shipping, but we delivered for our customer.

Did I want to scream at the shipping company rep? Sure. Did I do it? Not on Saturday night. We had a crisis and our focus had to be on doing what we had to do to protect our customer's event. Dealing with the shipping company would—and did—come later.

As the leader, you're the face of crisis management and you have to be visible and working until it's resolved. A few years ago (pre-COVID) we were doing an event in Las Vegas. I'd flown in that morning from the east coast. Things were going great, it was about ten o'clock at night, the client had finished their rehearsals, and most of our crew had been released. The only people left in the room were one of my account guys, the client's technical director, and me. That's when we discovered one of our cameras wasn't working.

About eight thousand people were due in that space at eight o'clock the following morning and that camera was critical to the show. It had to be fixed.

It took us more than three hours to figure out the problem and get the camera functioning. We had to call in the facility's union workers to climb into the fifty-foot-high rafters and change out cables. We woke up people from our crew and had them come down to help. It was quite a production.

At one point, I told the client's technical director he could leave, that we were going to get it working and I wouldn't leave until it was done. He said he wasn't leaving, either. When we finally got it done and were sure the camera was working, I'd been up for more than twenty-two hours and could barely keep my eyes open. I was drained. And I and our crew had to be back on site at seven o'clock to get ready for the show, giving a whole new meaning to the term power nap.

But the client and I bonded in our exhaustion, the event went off as planned, and we delivered the exceptional results we promised.

Leadership in Action: Gary Kelly

Gary Kelly joined Southwest Airlines in 1986, giving him a front-row seat to founder Herb Kelleher's legendary leadership style. He quickly rose to CFO then CEO , then became chairman and CEO in 2008 when Kelleher stepped down.

In a 2017 interview, Kelly said, "The CEO is in a high-profile role and sets an example. I try to aspire to set a good one, and model the behaviors that we value and expect at Southwest Airlines."

Kelly is a collaborative leader who will step up and make sacrifices when necessary. In 2020, as the airline industry reeled from the pandemic, Kelly made this announcement:

"Our Southwest Warriors have done everything we have asked, and you all have performed magnificently. You are our heroes, and now it's time to do what must be done to save Southwest Airlines. Effectively immediately, my already reduced based salary will be $0, and that will continue through the end of 2021. Other executives have also had their base pay reduced by 20% through 2021. Now we are a team, and more than that, we are a family, and it will take all of us to get through this. We all need to pitch in and do our part. We all need to sacrifice more."

Among Kelly's strong leadership qualities is his ability to recognize and embrace the need for change. He listens to both employees and customers, saying, "Innovative ideas come from the front line, and I want our leaders to be imaginative and bold and not just incremental. For that, they have to listen to people intently and purposefully."

After we got back to the office, we debriefed and put in safeguards to avoid a repeat of the situation.

Steps for Managing a Crisis

An important point to remember about crises is this: You won't have the exact same crisis twice. Sometimes they'll be similar, often they'll be totally different. But when a crisis hits, no matter what it is, a swift response is critical. Here's the process I use:

1. Step back and define it. What happened, why is it a crisis, and what's the impact on your organization? You need the nature and the size and scale of the crisis before you can formulate a response.

2. Review your options. It's a rare situation that has only one solution. Determine which one is most feasible.

3. Make a decision. You may not have all the information you'd like to have, but in a crisis, you don't have time to waste. Use what you know and act on it.

4. Take action. Put together a plan and implement it. The failure of leadership is when you don't act. You might not always make the best choice, but if you vacillate and do nothing, the crisis will win.

5. If possible, take steps to prevent a reoccurrence. Once the crisis is over, figure out how to keep it from happening again.

In a crisis, great leaders rise to the occasion and instill confidence. They don't react, they respond. They know how to say, "We got this!" with both words and actions to make the people affected by the situation feel comfortable that it's under control.

Understand that people react to crises differently. Some stay calm, others panic. Some are able to formulate an action plan, others throw their hands up because they can't figure out what to do, but they can follow instructions. As the leader, you must know your people, recognize their strengths and weaknesses, and act accordingly.

Get your leaders working on the plan and your followers taking the appropriate actions.

A critical part of leading through a crisis is communication. Even when the message is not good, you have to share what's happening with the people who are affected. You have to let them know what you're doing to mitigate and manage the situation. During the COVID shutdown, we were operating with the best current view in an extremely fluid environment. Things were changing almost from day to day, and it was important that our employees knew what was happening. To keep them updated, I sent out weekly videos. Those videos were difficult to make, especially when I had bad news to share. I tried to keep them positive and upbeat, but I knew the essential thing was to communicate as honestly and completely as I could.

Because of ETP's position as an industry leader, I decided to also reach outside our company with information. I created a podcast, *The Road Ahead*, to talk about the future of live events. It was important for there to be a voice of optimism during those challenging days, so I invited other industry leaders and subject matter experts to join me in conversations about a wide range of issues. What started as part of our crisis communication plan has evolved into a popular ongoing industry resource. You can listen to all the episodes at LesGoldberg.com/podcasts.

You also have to listen, not just to a few people, but to everyone on your team and to people outside your organization. You don't have to agree with what they're saying, but you have to hear it. You might find that some people blame you for things that are out of your control and knowing that gives you the opportunity to explain things and help those people understand what's really happening. Remember that in a crisis, your people may be afraid. Listen to them and help them deal with their fears.

The response of Johnson & Johnson when someone laced Tylenol with potassium cyanide in Chicago in 1982 is a classic lesson in how to respond to a crisis. The company issued an immediate product recall, alerted consumers to not consume any Tylenol product, and established relations with the Chicago Police Department, the FBI, and the Food and Drug Administration. J&J's chairman, James Burke,

Leadership in Action: Todd Beamer

When Todd Beamer boarded United Airlines flight 93 on September 11, 2001, he was expecting to spend the day in routine meetings and return home to his pregnant wife and young sons that night on a red-eye flight. Instead, he found himself stepping up and demonstrating remarkable leadership when hijackers took over the plane.

Beamer's leadership skills developed at an early age. Growing up, he excelled at soccer, basketball, and baseball. Injuries from an automobile crash in college ended his dream of becoming a professional baseball player, but he continued to play and was captain of the baseball team in college. After earning his MBA, he was climbing the corporate ladder, enjoying a rich family life, and serving his church and community.

After the hijackers herded the passengers to the rear of the aircraft, Beamer, along with Mark Bingham, Tom Burnett, and Jeremy Glick, formed a plan to take the plane back. Unfortunately, their plan couldn't save the people on flight 93, but it saved countless other lives and priceless landmarks.

On a call with a GTE airphone supervisor, Beamer said, "If I don't make it, please call my family and let them know how much I love them." Then he was heard speaking to the other passengers: "Are you ready? Okay. Let's roll!" A short time later, the plane crashed upside down into an empty field in Shanksville, Pennsylvania, killing everyone on board.

Beamer's heroism and courage have made him a legend and etched the phrase "Let's roll!" into the American lexicon forever.

formed a strategy team with the first priority of protecting people. The team established toll-free hotlines for consumers and the press. Burke held press conferences and appeared on various television shows to share the company's message. Within six months, Johnson & Johnson introduced tamper-resistant packaging and eventually recovered its market share and position as a trusted brand.

Is your company likely to face a crisis like the Tylenol product-tampering murders? Probably not. But even a minor incident can do a lot of damage if it's not handled well. That's why you need to develop yourself as a leader and your organization's crisis response systems during non-crisis times.

SOMETIMES YOU HAVE TO SACRIFICE

Leaders may need to make decisions that aren't good for them personally but that are good for the organization. You just have to take it on the chin and keep going. You have to show your people that you're willing to make sacrifices.

For a year during the pandemic, I cut my salary to about forty cents a week. It would have been zero, but I had to pay myself something to keep my insurance benefits. One of our executives had already taken a pay cut. He came to me and said, "If you can't pay me, that's okay. I'll keep working." There are no words to describe how that made me feel, but I told him no. He had to get paid.

Not everyone was on board with pay cuts. They weren't willing to make a temporary sacrifice to help the company survive. As the leader, I had to decide how to deal with that.

Sometimes a crisis brings out the best in people, sometimes it brings out the worst. Be prepared to be surprised.

A NEW KIND OF CRISIS

I'm a naturally high-energy person. I have a positive attitude and I have a lot of fun when I'm working, no matter how challenging the situation is. But when there is a legitimate crisis, I immediately stop and engage every member of my team in finding a solution.

On May 22, 2017, I was on my way home with plans to go out to dinner with my wife when my phone rang. It was the head of our touring department calling to tell me there had been an explosion at the Ariana Grande Dangerous Woman Tour at the Manchester Arena. The blast occurred at one of the arena's busiest exits. Within five minutes, our team had left the building and was on the crew bus, safe and moving away from the chaos.

Later we would learn that twenty-two people, including children, were killed and more than eight hundred others were injured (one hundred and sixteen seriously) in the blast. The Islamist extremist suicide bomber also died.

Demonstrating amazing courage and leadership, Ariana Grande returned to Manchester eleven days later to visit wounded fans and the families of those who died, and then to perform at One Love Manchester, a concert she organized to benefit the victims and their families.

As the world reacted in shock, we had to deal with a range of behind-the-scenes logistics. For a few days, we didn't know if the rest of the tour would be canceled. It wasn't, but we had some modifications to make. Also, we had barely more than a week to prepare for the One Love Manchester concert. Like everyone else, we were inspired by Ariana Grande's bravery and did what we had to do to help make the statement that we weren't going to let terrorism win.

When the immediate crisis was under control, we asked our insurance company if we had coverage for something like that. It hadn't occurred to us before, but now we have terrorist coverage—a practical lesson we learned from an unspeakable tragedy.

We don't spend a lot of time dwelling on what can go wrong at gatherings, but when something does, we've learned to respond calmly and effectively. We didn't have a crew on the main stage at the deadly 2021 Astroworld Festival in Houston, but we were doing the exhibit for a famous sports brand's booth in a side pavilion. Our customer closed their booth early because the crowd was too rowdy, so our crew wasn't on site when concert goers rushed the stage. Ten people were killed and hundreds injured in the stampede. As with

Leadership in Action: John F. Kennedy

A multifaceted leader, John F. Kennedy was intelligent and driven. He was the first President born in the twentieth century, and the youngest elected U.S. President, known for his charm and charisma.

Kennedy was a gifted orator who chose his words carefully. He was a visionary who wasn't satisfied with the status quo. He had an autocratic streak. Though advisors and aids provided him with information so he could make what he thought were the best choices, when it came time for the final decision, he demanded compliance.

As a leader, he reportedly remained cool in the face of difficult decisions. He inspired people with his eloquent speeches. He was willing to fight for new government programs to help the poor, the elderly, and the ill. One of the last acts of his presidency and life was to send a civil rights bill to Congress—a bill that would be passed as the landmark Civil Rights Act of 1964.

Because his life was cut short by an assassin's bullet in 1963, we don't know what his ultimate leadership legacy might have been. But leaders have been and will continue to be inspired by his words.

"The problems of the world cannot possibly be solved by skeptics or cynics whose horizons are limited by the obvious realities. We need men who can dream of things that never were and ask 'why not?'"

the Ariana Grande tour but on a smaller scale, we had to deal with unexpected logistics issues for our company and our client. We were able to do that by following our crisis management steps.

One of the worst leadership mistakes you can make is to think you've seen it all and you've got a plan for every situation. There will always be something new. But if you have a good team and systems in place, you'll be able to survive almost any crisis.

JUST WHEN YOU THINK THE CRISIS IS OVER

There are some crises that are clearly short-lived. They happen, you deal with them, and you move on. In our industry, that might be a truck that breaks down on the way to a show or an essential member of the road crew that gets sick at the last minute. In a restaurant, it could be running out of an essential ingredient for the most popular dish. Then there are longer-term crises, such as major economic downtowns and large-scale natural or man-made disasters, such as earthquakes or terrorist attacks. While these last longer, you can usually see an end and you know what you have to do to get there.

But then there are the totally unpredictable crises that have no points of comparison, are impossible to prepare for, and seem to have no end—like a pandemic. In the early days of the COVID pandemic, we were forced to drastically shrink our staff, something we'd never had to do before. Letting those great people go was painful, but we did what we had to do to for the company to survive.

So when the people gathering business began reopening, it should have been easy to ramp back up to pre-pandemic levels, right? Wrong. In one thirty-day period, we had to fill 5,600 positions for live events. That's not a typo—we had to find five thousand, six hundred people when the unemployment rate was at a record low and many of the people we wanted—the best people—weren't available because they were booked in advance. Thirty days later, we had to find and hire 1,400 more. And even then, we were turning down business. I felt like I was in a hurricane that had stalled over me because, as the world went back to live, *everyone* wanted to do an event. And COVID was still an issue.

My point is: You'd think reopening after the pandemic shutdowns was the end of the COVID crisis, but it wasn't—the crisis just took a different shape. There were still plenty of related challenges. And it wasn't just in the people gathering business—it was everywhere. For example, when COVID hit, companies had to pivot to function in the new environment. While we began working in the online event space, a number of manufacturers shifted from whatever they had been making to making personal protective equipment (PPE), hand sanitizer, masks, and other items that were suddenly in high demand. As pandemic restrictions were lifted, those companies had to pivot again, and for some, it created new crises as they repositioned themselves in the marketplace.

I'm infinitely proud of the way our team handled everything, but the end of the shutdowns didn't mean a return to the pre-pandemic style of operating. A key part of leading through a crisis is recognizing the potential for innovating and reinventing ourselves for the new normal.

THE IMPACT OF A CRISIS ON YOUR CUSTOMERS

Be sure to consider the impact a crisis has on your customers. Sometimes a crisis will change what they need. Be aware of that and be ready to lead through it. For example, when our customers couldn't meet in person during the pandemic, they still needed to meet, so we had to help them do it virtually.

Another angle on this point is when your customers are experiencing a crisis that isn't directly affecting you. A basic sales technique is to find out how your product will solve a problem your customer has. During a crisis, that's not just good selling, it's essential for building and maintaining your relationship. Find the new problems your customers are having and come up with ways to solve them.

NOT A TIME FOR LONG-TERM PLANNING

Avoid making long-term decisions in the middle of a crisis. The pandemic is a textbook example. In the early days of the shutdown, maybe March or April of 2020, I was talking to a friend of mine who is a doctor, and I asked him, "When is this going to end?

He said, "Give it until June."

Almost two years later, I asked, "Did you mean June of 2020? Or 2021? 2022?"

During the pandemic, our approach wasn't quite one day at a time, but we were definitely operating in a "deal with the present" mindset because we didn't know what tomorrow was going to bring. We were confident that in-person gatherings would return, but we didn't know when. We didn't know how many of our customers would want to continue holding virtual meetings even after it was safe to gather in person. So we couldn't plan for how we would operate much beyond a few months. We just knew we had to handle the business we had with the flawless execution our customers expected and be ready for whatever might happen.

Of course, this flies in the face of conventional wisdom about the importance of strategic planning. You absolutely need those long-term objectives and a clear plan to guide you in reaching them. But when you're in the middle of a crisis, there are too many unknowns for you to create good long-term plans. The best strategy is to focus on what's immediately essential and wait until things settle down before planning too far into the future.

In a crisis, your primary goal is to get to tomorrow. Put the fire out, make necessary short-term decisions, and wait for certainty before you do any long-range planning.

LET THE CRISES MAKE YOU STRONGER

Our company has faced many crises over the years, and I'm proud that no matter how dark things looked at the time, we came out of all of them better and stronger. We found ways to overcome weaknesses. Ultimately we became a better, stronger company as we forged ahead.

Chapter Eight

What Gets You Going?

To perform at their peak, people need inspiration and education. Education teaches you how to do something. Inspiration makes you believe it's possible. And when those two elements work together, it's motivation. Motivation is important when things are running smoothly; it's absolutely essential in a crisis.

I want everyone who works at ETP in any capacity to see their work as more than a job, more than a paycheck. I want people who *want* to be here. I want people who want to be part of something that's bigger than the thing they actually do. Understanding and being committed to the company's purpose generates the energy that drives the outcome. It's my responsibility as the leader to inspire people so they are motivated to embrace the bigger picture. It's also my responsibility to make sure the necessary training programs are in place so our employees know how to serve our customers with flawless execution.

Where do you find inspiration?

Effective leaders know where their inspiration is so they can go there when they need to.

Once I was in a meeting with one of my teams and I asked, "Why do you think I come here and meet with you?"

One person said, "Because you want us to know what's going on with you." No, that's not it.

Another person said, "You come here to inspire us. You've done some amazing things in your life, and you want us to know that we can, too."

That's a big part of it. I want to be an inspiration for all the people I come in contact with. But equally important to me personally is that I find being with my teams inspiring. I'm energized by the people I work with, and I want them to feel the same way.

Inspiration is everywhere, it's just a matter of attitude. You can find inspiration simply by going for a walk, spending time with your family or pets, trying something new (even if you're not sure you can do it), teaching, exploring, doing a favor for someone, or even indulging yourself. I find inspiration in watching what's going on in the world and figuring out how I can be a part of as many things as I can—with the caveat that those things must fit into my wheelhouse. I find inspiration in technology. I'm a geek, so when I see something super cool, I automatically go into the mode of: How can we deploy this? How can we use it in ways that maybe its creators hadn't thought of?

Learn to recognize what inspires you so you can tap into it when you need to. It comes down to your attitude and how you see the world. You can be inspired in so many ways if you're just open to it.

COACHING AND MANAGING

It takes successful individuals to build successful teams. As a leader, you're responsible for helping the people on your teams grow personally and professionally, as individuals and as team members.

Every great leader is a great coach. Coaching is an integral part of getting people to perform at their highest level. It's easiest to see how this works by looking at sports. Every superstar sports player, every winning team has an effective coach—a coach who knows how to take a group of good people and turn them into something great.

There's a big difference between managing and coaching. Managing people is not fun. It's one of the toughest things to do because people in general don't like to be managed. But if you can inspire your people, managing becomes easier.

Managing people is about technique. It's making sure they know what's expected of them and how to do what you need them to do. It involves praise and discipline. Managers train workers, assign tasks, monitor and evaluate progress, implement executive decisions, address problems and conflict situations, and respond to emergencies. Essentially, they make sure that people are doing their jobs and the operation is running smoothly. But if you're going to be a leader, you need to do more than manage.

Coaching is not as easy to define as management is. Coaching people is about helping people to figure out and follow the right path for themselves. It's about developing them, and it's a key element of leadership.

Coaches improve employee performance, increase employee engagement, provide constructive feedback, and guide employees through their professional development. Effective coaching improves work autonomy, critical thinking skills, attitude, and overall performance.

Managing is directive and task-oriented; it's essentially a one-way communication from the manager to the worker. This is not to say that managers don't listen—they should and the good ones do. We're talking about the general process here. By contrast, coaching focuses on growth; it's a two-way communication as the coach asks questions, listens to the answers, and guides and supports the worker.

Managing is about getting the work done. Coaching is about developing your people.

In business, successful entrepreneurs know they have to be effective coaches and they work on developing their coaching skills.

Leadership in Action: Amelia Earhart

The iconic Amelia Earhart succeeded in breaking aviation records, advancing the public acceptance of aviation, and overcoming barriers for women in all areas of life.

Confident and determined, Earhart was a quintessential rule breaker. She never acquiesced to the traditional gender roles of her time. She was born in 1897 and, while growing up, played basketball, collected bugs, and even built a roller coaster of sorts at the family's home. She took auto repair classes and attended college, something not many women did back then. She was in her twenties when she began flying lessons.

One of the key roles of a leader is to inspire others, and Earhart's achievements during the 1930s did exactly that then and continue to do so today. From being the first woman passenger on a transatlantic flight to the first person to pilot a plane across both the Atlantic and the Pacific, the charismatic Earhart was a national hero.

Earhart's path to success was not a smooth one but she persevered. Growing up with an alcoholic father made her childhood challenging. As an adult, she worked as a teacher and a social worker, but her passion for aviation never waned. She eventually became a sales representative for Kinner airplanes in the Boston area and wrote articles promoting flying.

Her attempt at being the first person to circumnavigate the earth around the equator ended prematurely when she and navigator Fred Noonan vanished over the Central Pacific Ocean. Their disappearance remains one of the greatest unsolved mysteries of the twentieth century.

There are plenty of business owners and managers who don't like to coach—they just want to tell other people what to do. That's definitely not coaching. It's also not effective management. Simply delivering instructions works with robots and it might work short-term in low-skilled, high-turnover environments. But good bosses don't boss people around, they incorporate coaching techniques into their management function.

Whether it's a lot or a little, each person only has a certain amount of energy. A great coach harnesses that energy and helps direct it to get people to perform at their highest level as individuals and as members of the team. This is an integral part of keeping people motivated. When I first started my business, I didn't understand this. Some people might do this instinctively, but for me, it was a learned skill.

As organizations get bigger and the founder gets further away from the front line, you have a responsibility to be constantly coaching your leadership so that they are coaching the people on their teams. It works down the line so that everyone is being coached and, in the process, learning how to coach.

BUILDING A CULTURE THAT EXCITES PEOPLE

Since the dawn of humankind, leaders have struggled with how to get the best out of people. Not to oversimplify it, but if you build a culture that excites people, that offers them opportunity and provides rewarding work that lets them have fun at the same time, you'll attract people who want to give their best.

The people who are part of Team ETP are here because they want to be. We're in an exciting industry and our company does really cool things. Our people are proud to be part of the team that does things that have wowed audiences. They're excited about and challenged by the work they do, by their contribution to the big picture.

For them, "good enough" is not okay. From top leadership down to entry-level employees, they share the philosophy that what we do is about delivering extraordinary experiences. Like me, they want to be exceptional. Like me, they want to do amazing things with amazing people. And they want jobs that offer rewards far beyond the basic salary and benefits package. It's the leader's job to make that happen.

Investopedia defines corporate culture as "the beliefs and behaviors that determine how a company's employees and management interact and handle outside business transactions. A company's culture will be reflected in its dress code, business hours, office setup, employee benefits, turnover, hiring decisions, treatment of clients, client satisfaction, and every other aspect of operations." All of that has a direct impact on your bottom line through increased productivity, efficiency, and employee retention, which all contribute to greater profits.

Culture is an essential part of supporting a company's goals and objectives. A big part of it is intangible—it's the feeling people get when they come into the building, it's the vibe among our crews when they're working together in the field. Leadership is about building a culture that supports the mission, vision, and values of the company.

There has to be a fit between your culture and your people. When your culture isn't a fit for someone, it doesn't matter how skilled or talented they are, it's not going to work. Someone who prefers a more formal environment is going to struggle in a culture that is casual and fun, and vice versa.

A few years ago, we decided to renovate our headquarters building in Orlando. It had been a traditional, stodgy, corporate-type facility, and Dave John decided it was time for an upgrade. I told him, "You can change anything you want, just don't touch my office." And let me tell you, he changed *everything!* I'm so glad he did. And after the rest of the building was transformed and looked amazing, then we changed my office.

We now have large and small meeting rooms that are web-conference enabled, so our people can work together across multiple offices. In addition, there are collaboration areas throughout the office, as well as spaces that allow our team members to relax during their breaks and get to know each other. The workstations are open and collaborative, but we have rooms for confidential client calls and one-on-one conversations. Beyond the technical and structural function, we have plenty of interesting decorative accents, including a plant wall and light fixtures made of slide projector carousels.

Not only does our office look super cool, it's made the employees feel better about where they work and they're more productive. In fact, we were a winner of *Orlando Business Journal's* 2019 Coolest Office Spaces.

Of course, physical environment is only a part of creating a positive culture that energizes your employees, sets you apart from the competition, and makes your customers feel good about doing business with you. Some of the other elements you'll want to consider and work on include:

Trust. You need a high level of trust throughout your organization. Leaders should set the example with high ethics, predictable behavior, and open, honest communication.

Listen. Listen to your people and encourage feedback. In addition to being the best way to identify situations that have the potential to become problems, your people will appreciate knowing that their input is valued.

Realistic goals. There's nothing wrong with setting the bar high, but your goals must be achievable, especially if they're tied to compensation. Goals that are impossible to reach are discouraging, not motivating.

Collaborate. Encourage collaboration, even between people whose functions may not appear to intersect and especially between people of various management levels. You'll likely be pleasantly surprised at the hidden talents that will flourish in a collaborative culture.

Leadership in Action: Michael Eisner

Michael Eisner is probably best known for his time as chief executive officer of the Walt Disney Company from 1984 to 2005. I've worked with him personally many times over the years. When Eisner joined Disney, he immediately had to deal with a leadership vacuum that had existed since Walt Disney's death in 1966 that had grown to crisis proportions.

Under Eisner, the company transitioned from paternalistic to professionally managed and financially strong.

While Eisner has been criticized for his micromanagement and autocratic leadership style, he is still enthusiastic and visionary, and his presence can electrify a room. At Disney, he was extraordinarily creative, quick to move on great ideas and toss bad ones without a second thought. He also depended on Frank Wells, then Disney's chief operating officer, to focus on the business side of those great ideas. Industry observers have noted that the two men were much stronger together than either was on his own.

One of Eisner's strongest leadership skills is his understanding that failure is a necessary part of success. He said:

"Success requires failure. I have always tried to make everyone aware that failure is not a corporate death sentence. Making the same mistake twice is seriously frowned upon, of course, but an intelligent stumble is nothing to be ashamed of. To punish failure is yet another way to encourage mediocrity because mediocrity is what fearful people will always settle for. ... If you want to discover inspired ideas, you simply have to accept that you will have to encounter more than a few that don't make the grade."

Recognition. You'll boost confidence and inspire loyalty by acknowledging and showing your appreciation of excellent work.

Inclusion. Everyone in your organization should have equal access to opportunities for advancement, training, and other resources.

Stress management. All kinds of issues can create stress in the workplace. Be proactive in finding ways to help your employees deal with stress, whether it's routine or caused by a crisis.

GETTING THE MOST OUT OF YOUR PEOPLE

One of the most challenging responsibilities of leaders is to keep their teams motivated, excited, and energized about their jobs—even when those jobs might not be particularly exciting. As a leader, you want the best out of your people. Realistically, that's not going to happen 100 percent of the time. People are not robots. They're not machines that will function consistently as long as you maintain them. They're human beings with families, friends, and interests outside of work. They may love their jobs and be committed to the company, but there's more to them than that.

You need to recognize the humanness of your team by creating a culture where people feel respected and cared about. And it has to be genuine—if your behind-the-scenes words and actions contradict your public statements about how valuable your people are, you'll get found out and the results won't be good. An example: Executives at an Applebee's franchisee engaged in an email chain where they all credited rising gas prices and the end of COVID-19 stimulus and employment benefits for an opportunity to hire more workers at lower wages. The emails were shared on social media. The clear contempt for hourly workers prompted all the managers at one location to quit, forcing the temporary closing of that restaurant. Of course, the corporate office issued a statement that talked about the importance of "team members," but the damage was done.

Knowing they matter for more than what they produce on the job makes people happy, and happy people perform better than unhappy people.

The concept is simple. The implementation is difficult.

Of course, you want to provide a safe working environment that is as comfortable as possible. That's why we do things like equip our offices with ergonomic furniture, have an air-conditioned warehouse, and make sure our road crews have the equipment and tools they need to do their jobs. You need to have the right compensation package for your people. You need to provide opportunities for growth and advancement. Lack of opportunity is a common reason people leave companies.

Everyone on the team needs to be in alignment. If you have ten people in a boat and nine of them are rowing in the same direction, but one is rowing backward, it's going to be tough to get that boat going where you want it to go at the speed you need to go. You need identify anyone on the team who is out of alignment and work to get them on board with everyone rowing in the same direction.

Sometimes that one person thinks they're helping you by complaining. They might think that their way is better and they're trying to prove it. It's certainly worth considering their position, but if they're wrong, you need to help them see it and bring them into alignment or let them go.

When everyone knows what they're supposed to do and how they're supposed to do it, they're in alignment. Alignment brings the most opportunity for efficiency, which in turn generates greater productivity. As John Maxwell says, teamwork makes the dream work.

WHAT MOTIVATES YOU?

I'm motivated to participate in things that have the potential of a great outcome, things that would make other people say, "Wow!"

When ETP helps an entertainer deliver a show filled with spectacle or a company deliver a message to reach their business goals, I'm jazzed. On a personal level, I'm motivated to do things that I know will make others happy. I'm motivated to maintain a healthy lifestyle because taking care of myself makes it possible for me to take care of

Leadership in Action: Nelson Mandela

A controversial figure for most of his life, denounced by both the right and the left, Nelson Mandela is globally regarded as an icon of democracy and social justice. His achievements would not have been possible had he not been a strong leader.

Mandela consistently demonstrated strong ethical values and had highly effective communication skills—two key attributes of great leaders. He was charismatic, transformational, and inspirational.

Though he was a humble man of peace, Mandela was not afraid to do whatever was necessary to achieve his goals. He said, "I learned that courage was not the absence of fear, but the triumph over it. I felt fear myself more times that I can remember, but I hid it behind a mask of boldness. The brave man is not he who does not feel afraid, but he who conquers that fear."

He was patient and had remarkable strength and stamina. He didn't care who got credit, saying, "It is better to lead from behind and to put others in front, especially when you celebrate victory when nice things occur. You take the front line when there is danger. Then people will appreciate your leadership."

He wasn't bitter, never sought revenge, and maintained a positive attitude. In his autobiography, he wrote, "I am fundamentally an optimist. Whether that comes from nature or nurture, I cannot say. Part of being optimistic is keeping one's head pointed toward the sun, one's feet moving forward. There were many dark moments when my faith in humanity was sorely tested, but I would not and could not give myself up to despair. That way lays defeat and death."

my family and team at ETP.

If you don't find something good behind whatever you're doing, it's hard to be motivated. Know what motivates you so you can keep it front and center in your life.

ON BEING A ROLE MODEL

Effective leaders are naturally positive role models. Other people look to them—sometimes consciously but often unconsciously—as someone to be emulated.

You don't have to be a celebrity, a superstar, or even a historical figure to be a role model. Parents, teachers, coaches, religious leaders, managers at all levels are role models because they influence people every day. Being a role model is a responsibility we should all take seriously.

I've had some amazing role models in my life, and I do my best to be a strong reflection of what they instilled in me. Throughout my life, when I've faced challenging situations, I pause and think to myself, what would some of the great leaders that I've worked with do? That not only helps me make good choices, it also gives me inspiration and ideas for how to solve problems.

Here are the characteristics of the role models I admire and how I've applied them to my life and business.

- **Integrity.** I believe in doing the right thing because it's the right thing, even when it may not be the thing that's most beneficial to me. Integrity includes honesty and transparency.
- **Positivity.** I'm a realistic optimist. I believe good things can and will happen.
- **Perseverance.** I don't give up. I fight through all the crazy challenges that life puts in front of me. I don't let failure stop me; I learn from what didn't work and do better the next time. As Maya Angelou said, "Do the best you can until you know

better. Then when you know better, do better."

- **Confidence.** I believe in myself and my abilities. I'm not arrogant; I know I have the ability to achieve if I focus my time and energy.
- **Consistency.** I walk my talk. I don't say one thing and do another. My actions match my words.
- **Respect.** I treat people with respect. I express gratitude and show concern for others; and I work to earn their respect.
- **Demand accountability.** I hold people accountable for what they do—and don't do.
- **Accept responsibility.** When I make a mistake, I admit it and do whatever it takes to make the situation right.
- **High expectations.** I set the bar high for myself and the people on my team.
- **Passion.** I have an intense, driving devotion to living life to the fullest, both personally and professionally.
- **Knowledgeable.** I never stop learning—that's why I surround myself with people who are smarter than I am.
- **Humility**. Though I'm confident, I'm humble at the same time. I don't suffer from a case of false pride.

I've been fortunate to have worked with thousands of great leaders who have served as role models for me over the years. I was definitely influenced by them a while back when we had a new client that was turning out to be problematic, to put it mildly. The trouble started before we had actually signed the contract, but we'd made the commitment to do the show and were doing some of the preliminary work. Several members of the team were in favor of walking away and, without a signed contract, we could have legally done it and we had plenty of other work at the time. But I said no. We made the commitment, we have to do it. Our integrity is on the line.

Walking away from this show would have been the easy thing to do, but it wasn't the right thing to do. Thanks to my role models, it's part of my DNA to honor my commitments.

You never know when someone is looking to you as a role model so always operate in a way that you'd be proud to have someone imitate.

Chapter Nine

Life as a Leader

I love being a leader most of the time, and if you've read this far, it's safe to say that you do, too. Whether you're an entrepreneur or an employee at any level, you have the opportunity to make a difference by developing and demonstrating your leadership skills.

Though leadership comes more naturally to some people than others, it's something anyone can learn. It's a skill that gets better with practice. We've talked about a lot of things great leaders do, the tactics and techniques you can adopt as you build your own abilities. Some you'll do intuitively; others you'll have to work on for them to become a habit. Allow yourself the time you need to develop your leadership skills so they're ingrained when you're faced with a crisis and need them. Forgive yourself when you make mistakes. And remember what James M. Kouzes said:

> *"In the end, leaders don't decide who leads. Followers do."*

Be the person people want to follow.

I'd like to offer some final thoughts on leadership.

Leadership in Action: Benjamin Franklin

During the American Revolution, Benjamin Franklin persuaded France to support American independence with critical troops, money, and supplies. For the French, it was a risky and expensive gamble that paid off when they helped the Continental Army defeat the British at Yorktown, where the British surrendered.

Being strategic and persuasive were just two of Franklin's many leadership traits. Even though he only had two years of formal schooling, he was a lifelong learner. A creative and determined problem-solver, his inventions and discoveries include the lightning rod, bifocals, swim fins, the Franklin stove, and a urinary catheter. He was curious, he took risks, and he believed in change.

In his autobiography, Franklin listed his thirteen virtues as:

1. Temperance. Eat not to dullness; drink not to elevation.
2. Silence. Speak not but what may benefit others or yourself; avoid trifling conversation.
3. Order. Let all your things have their places; let each part of your business have its time.
4. Resolution. Resolve to perform what you ought; perform without fail what you resolve.
5. Frugality. Make no expense but to do good to others or yourself; i.e., waste nothing.
6. Industry. Lose no time; be always employ'd in something useful; cut off all unnecessary actions.
7. Sincerity. Use no hurtful deceit; think innocently and justly, and, if you speak, speak accordingly.
8. Justice. Wrong none by doing injuries, or omitting the benefits that are your duty.
9. Moderation. Avoid extremes; forbear resenting injuries so much as you think they deserve.
10. Cleanliness. Tolerate no uncleanliness in body, cloaths, or habitation.

11. Tranquillity. Be not disturbed at trifles, or at accidents common or unavoidable.

12. Chastity. Rarely use venery but for health or offspring, never to dullness, weakness, or the injury of your own or another's peace or reputation.

13. Humility. Imitate Jesus and Socrates.

TWO IMPORTANT QUESTIONS

Every leader needs to be able to answer two critical questions:

What are you willing to do to get what you want?

What are you *not* willing to do to get what you want?

I'm willing to work hard and take calculated risks. I'm willing to make the effort to study and learn what I need to know to get the results I want. I'm willing to lose money to do the right thing.

I'm not willing to do anything that's dishonest or violates my ethics. I'm not willing to sacrifice my relationship with my family. I'm not willing to give up my self-respect.

When you have clear, concise answers to these two questions, everything else will fall into place and you have the foundation necessary to be an outstanding leader.

STRESS MANAGEMENT IS CRITICAL

Stress is a natural part of being a leader. No matter how much you love what you do, there are going to be times—plenty of them—when you'll be stressed. It can either eat you alive or work for you. Learn how to make stress work for you.

We all deal with frustration and stress in our own way. Some people work out, some people drink, smoke, or eat to excess, some people lose themselves in their hobbies. You have to figure out what works for you, what will keep you healthy and balanced, and make sure you do it.

Avoid complacency

When things are going well, don't get too comfortable or complacent. Don't let yourself get lazy. Enjoy those good times, expect the best, maintain your sense of optimism, but never completely let your guard down.

Keep getting better

Even though you're the leader, you're on top and in charge, there's always room for personal improvement. Never stop looking for ways to make yourself better. Learn from everything. Get feedback from your team.

Here's an important tip for getting useful feedback: Don't ask, "How did I do at that?"—"that" being whatever the situation was. Most people will tell you what you did well. As much as we love positive reinforcement, you'll get more valuable input if you ask, "What could I do better?"

When you're asking for feedback, keep it focused. If you ask someone how you can improve at being the president of the company, they're going to have a hard time coming up with an answer. But if you ask what you could have done better in a specific situation, you'll get input you can use.

Embrace change

Don't just accept change, welcome it. In our industry, the most visible change is how technology has enhanced performances and even basic business meetings. It's created opportunities for us that we couldn't imagine a decade ago.

Another notable change in our business is that the level of security on concert tours has increased significantly. We're seeing metal detectors, drug dogs, greater police presence—things designed to make it safer for both the artists and the audiences. While it's unfortunate that these things are necessary, we respect and appreciate them for the protection they provide.

When you stop changing and growing, you start stagnating. Stagnation leads to decline and ultimately to failure.

Stick to your principles

Know what your principles are and stick to them. It's not always easy, but it's always worth it. I've spent more than few sleepless nights knowing that if I were willing to compromise just a little and bend my personal rules, I could make a lot of money or enjoy some other benefit. And maybe no one else would get hurt. But I know what's right and what's wrong, and I'm committed to always doing what I know to be the right thing, even when it costs me.

I believe that if you know what your principles are and you stick to them, you'll always be successful in the end. You may have short-term failure or challenges, but you'll get past them and it will be worth it. And you'll be able to sleep at night.

Focus on the future

Certainly we need to learn from the past. But the world is changing too much, too fast for us to make history our primary source for answers and inspiration. Don't spend a lot of time looking back. The answers that worked even a few years ago may not work today. Be a visionary. Look to the future for the solutions you need now.

Remember that the last pandemic, the Spanish Flu pandemic of 1918, was followed by the Roaring Twenties. Of course, the end of World War I played a key role in that decade of unprecedented prosperity and a lot of financial and regulatory missteps contributed to the crash in 1929. My point is not to do an in-depth historical analysis, but to remind you that economic cycles are a reality. No matter how bad things get, at some point, they'll get good again.

Ignore the doomsayers. Given enough time, they'll always be proven wrong. During the COVID-19 pandemic, I asked a colleague what he thought the future of the live event gathering business was going to be. He said, "Well, when the internet came out, everyone thought it would kill all of this, that all the gatherings would be done through the internet. That didn't happen. We survived the internet, and we'll survive the pandemic. It's just a matter of how long it's going to take for things to run their course, for us to figure out what the new normal is going to be."

Prepare your company for the future. For an organization to succeed, regardless of its function or mission, it needs strong leadership to set the course and keep people on track. Great leaders will emerge from the downturn we experienced in 2020 and 2021. As you identify these natural leaders in your organization, invest in them, cultivate them, and watch them soar.

When I look at our company, I see a smart, strong, and fast organization that's going to be smarter, stronger, and faster. We've learned new things and adapted technology so that we're better, more agile, and more prepared for the challenges and opportunities that are ahead. And I give all the credit to the amazing leadership team that has supported me and guided ETP through some of most turbulent times in modern history.

I believe in the strength of the human spirit. When you've had a bad day—and they happen!—go to sleep knowing that when you wake up, it will be a whole new day and you get to start over. As long as the sun comes up, you can overcome any obstacle and do great things. The show must—and will—go on.

Acknowledgments

Thanking everyone who contributed to *The Show Must Go On* would be a book itself and an impossible task, but there are some special people I want to mention.

First, to the people and institutions who thought we would fail: Thank you for motivating me to find solutions to every challenge that came my way. The roadblocks you threw up became steppingstones to success.

Now, to the people who believed and continue to believe in what we're doing, my deepest thanks and great appreciation go out to:

Every member of the ETP team. You were great before the pandemic, but when things got tough, your efforts were tougher. You will always have my sincere gratitude for all you have done.

My wife Julie and our three kids Sydney, Lindsey, and Hunter, who every day help me realize the importance of having an amazing family.

David John, ETP's Chief Operating Officer, whose commitment and dedication to the ETP family of companies is unwavering.

Stacy Teal, my trusted assistant, who not only puts up with me, but often stays a step ahead of what I am thinking.

Jacquelyn Lynn, who told me in the early days of the pandemic to keep notes because there was a book here, and then helped me craft and produce it.

Finally, I must acknowledge you, the reader, because you are the ultimate driving force behind this book and its message about leadership. Thank you.

Les M. Goldberg

ABOUT LES M. GOLDBERG

Les M. Goldberg's professional titles include founder, chief executive officer, president, and chairman, but a more accurate description is that he is the driving force behind one of the entertainment technology services industry's leading players.

He started LMG in 1984 at the age of 17 with a $5,000 loan from his grandfather. LMG has grown from a small video equipment rental operation in Orlando to a global leader in live and virtual events, concert touring, and systems integration.

In 2014, Les created Entertainment Technology Partners (ETP), a parent company to a collection of exceptional brands in the industry. ETP's first acquisition was LMG, and has grown to include brands EventEQ, Systems Innovation, and Pixl Evolution, with locations in the United States and Europe. Under his guidance, the company has implemented a strategic plan that supports its brands as they take their performance to ever-higher levels, supporting clients across the globe with extraordinary technology solutions.

Les is the author of *The Show Must Go On: The Art of Leading During a Crisis*, *When All the Stars Align: Create a Life Where Great Things Happen*, and *Don't Take No for An Answer: Anything is Possible*. He also hosts the podcast *The Road Ahead, a Discussion of the Current State of the Live Events Industry*. In addition to being an industry leader and active in the community, Les is a devoted family man to his wife and three children.

Connect with Les M. Goldberg

Visit Les's website, read his blog:
www.LesGoldberg.com

Connect with Les on LinkedIn:
www.linkedin.com/in/lesmgoldberg

Follow Les on Twitter
www.twitter.com/LES_GOLDBERG

Les M. Goldberg

Don't Take
No for an
Answer

Anything is Possible

*How one entrepreneur dreamed big
and made it happen.*

It's a success story that makes you want to stand up and cheer: Les M. Goldberg started his company at 17 as a way to make money doing something he loved while he was going to college. That small operation has grown into a multi-million-dollar entertainment technology industry leader.

In *Don't Take No for an Answer*, Les Goldberg uses wit and wisdom to tell the tale of his phenomenal success and share the techniques and tactics that have worked for him—and will work for you.

Available at your favorite online book retailer.

WHEN ALL

THE

STARS ALIGN

Create a Life Where Great Things Happen

LES M. GOLDBERG

The phrase "when the stars align" means that things have come together just right. Is it chance? Luck? An accident? Divine intervention?

None of the above. Les M. Goldberg says we can make the stars align for ourselves so we wake up every morning feeling like we've won the lottery. Goldberg has distilled decades of experience and accumulated wisdom in this uplifting guide. Easy to read and packed with practical advice, *When All the Stars Align* delivers step-by-step instructions on how to turn the rich, fulfilling life of your dreams into reality.

Available from your favorite online book retailer.

Invite
Les M. Goldberg
to Speak at Your
Next Event

Beyond his passion for his own business, Les is passionate about entrepreneurship and enjoys sharing his expertise with a variety of audiences ranging from business students to corporate executives.

To invite him to speak at your next event, please contact: admin@lesgoldberg.com.

ENTERTAINMENT
TECHNOLOGY PARTNERS

Entertainment Technology Partners (ETP) is the parent company to a collection of exceptional brands in the live event and entertainment technology services industry. Our shared philosophy embraces a distinctive approach to quality, service, and support.

We are integrated industry leaders driven by client relationships and focused on the goal of building and growing business. We're relentlessly looking for new and innovative ways to do it, be it a new technology or a more efficient way to better serve our customers.

ETP provides the platform to facilitate growth through strategic alliances, expanded assets, value creation and geographic reach. Our markets include corporate events and conventions, concert tours, fixed installations, theater, television and film, and special events.

To learn more about ETP, please visit us online at ETP.net or email info@ETP.net.

Made in the USA
Columbia, SC
03 November 2022

3dda7259-5fdc-4223-8dc3-fa02e4ad1ff4R01